BACK to EDEN

Ade OMOOBA

ISBN: 978-978-765-686-0
Imprint: Ade OMOOBA

DEDICATION

This work is dedicated to this generation and generations to come.

Table of Contents

You're appreciated

To everyone who contributed in one way or another to make this project possible, especially my immediate family who stood by me these past few months. Ayo, my son, you once came to me to ask if I wasn't tired writing for 12 straight hours because you had been waiting for when I would finish so that we can play together.

I appreciate you, Jesse. I honour you our mother, my wife.

This wouldn't have been possible without you.

And most importantly the HolySpirit.

Intro:

The Perfect World

I n the beginning, before Time began, GOD created all the Planets and left them inchoate for an indeterminate period. Among the Planets, this Earth was deliberately chosen to be the home for all living things. The choice was made even before creation began, because: positionally (in relation to the Sun, the Moon, Jupiter, the milky way); structurally (Size, Shape, Weight, Atmospheric condition, Orbit and Rotation), materially (outer core, inner core, Ozone layer, Water), characteristically (temperature, stable orbiting and rotation, atmospheric pressure); this earth was purposefully built to support life.

There's no doubt that the universe is made by a deliberate profound mind

Big Bang theory is a lazy way of explaining off the hands behind everything we see because the hand seems too sophisticated and meticulous for us to understand.

In all chaos, there's a cosmos, in all disorder, a secret order.

Nothing Is Without Its Purpose

The basis for every creation is the Purpose for which it's created. GOD did not tell us why HE created certain things but research has shown that nothing is without its place in creation.

Without this seemingly 'meaningless creation', our world would not be what it is today. From the most minute microorganisms to the behemoth whale in the sea; each depends on the other for living, and GOD, puts Man as the head of this self-sustaining, self-regenerating, self-regulating, and self-renewing nature, to keep, dress, and dominate.

Remove the supposed inconsequential organism; you will see that: our food cycle, the chain of life, the fabric that holds the world together, would no longer be able to sustain life.
As infinitesimal as bacteria are, they help balance our ecosystem by aiding in, decomposing dead matter. Without the burdensome insects pollinating our crops, I am not sure we will have this much food to eat as we have today. Look at the earthworms: weak, slow, fragile, yet, they not only add nutrients to our soil, they also aerate the soil, helping in erosion control.

Until you go far away from where the feet of men trod, in the place, where animals are left to roam freely, you'd not understand the thoughtfulness of the food cycle. Goat, Cow, Sheep and other herbivores, graze on the grass for sustenance, defecating thereon for microorganism in the soil to feed on, thereby, giving back nutrients that the grass depends on. These animals are themselves mauled by wild beasts to keep their number within the limit the environment can cater for. With time, the wild beast would die and the carcass becomes food for the weakest in the food chain and the cycle continues without our intervention.

This is too sophisticated and too delicate for any randomness to concoct let alone sustain.

The Misconception About Creation

The account of creation in Genesis 1, had been misinterpreted to mean that the first thing GOD created during this creation was light. No, Light had always existed before then.

Everything in our universe then: was still, no motion, no activity, just frozen in space. The Sun was beaming its sunshine but the Moon was in-between the Sun and the Earth thus casting darkness on Earth.

When GOD said 'Let there be light; GOD was not creating light, GOD was creating Time, our Time. GOD was telling the Moon, the Earth and everything in the universe to start orbiting and rotating. There was evening and morning, the First day. This is how our 24 hours a day came into being. Before then, it was more than a speed of light, a time so massive that our 1000 years is like a second to it.

Another misconception of the account of creation in Genesis is that nothing existed before Genesis 1.
Our planets (which includes the Earth and other planets or heavens as the Bible puts it) had existed before Genesis 1. It had existed long before Genesis, that the Bible simply described when as - the beginning.

When is this beginning the Bible is referring to? It could be from a few years to trillions of our years.
Assuming GOD created the planets Billions of years before Genesis; for GOD to still be able to come back to where HE left it off, shows the highest level of organization, planning, efficiency, and vision. It shows that God did not create us ad-lib. It is not a spur of the moment, not a drive for creativity nor as a result of being bored. It took GOD careful, meticulous and fail-proof planning Gen. 2 verses 5 and 6.

It is thought-provoking that, GOD; after creating the universe, had to wait for years before creating life on this earth. GOD couldn't have created Life when HE had not created their sustenance (plant and vegetation). GOD couldn't have created sustenance when HE had not created Man to keep and dress it.
No wonder Paul by the Spirit said in Rom. 8 vs.19 that every creature awaits the manifestation of the sons of God.

Now you know. You are created for a reason. You are a human being for a purpose. You are not a product of evolution nor the outcome of your parent's copulation. It is not me that is saying it; it is embedded in the ink that is used to write the Bible. It is laid as the foundation upon which this earth is built. It is written deep inside the eyes of every creature. You will see it if you can go deep into you. If you can unravel the many layers of deceits and conditioning you have subjected your heart to.

It is for this reason that GOD took an uncountable number of years after HE had created the planets before HE was ready to create you and me. It is, for this same reason that among the many planets there is, God chose this earth to be our home.

Had GOD created Man on Jupiter, would we have survived? Absolutely no. That place is too far from the Sun and the oxygen level there is very low. Aside from that, Jupiter, which is more than 10 times the size of this Earth, takes about 10 hours to spin around its axis meaning that, this speed creates a blast of atmospheric activities. Jupiter does not even have a solid surface like the Earth to start with and its magnetic force is so strong that it can crush spacecraft. The most spectacular thing about this planet is it acts as the guardian angel to our earth by absorbing many meteors that could have hit and destroyed our earth.

Living on the Moon is unsustainable. The weather could be as erratic as being beyond extreme. It could vary between -170⁰ degrees and 80⁰ degrees within 24 hours. We'd also be prepared to live 14 days straight of daylight and 14 days of pitch darkness. The average temperature on Earth is 15⁰c. Compare that to 465⁰ on Venus and -224⁰ on Uranus or Pluto at -225⁰.

You can see that GOD knew exactly what HE was doing. GOD had a plan of what HE wanted to see. HE intricately and delicately sets this Earth; HE connects each fiber of creation to support life that has Man at the center.

5 levels of Creation

The Bible implicitly revealed 5 phases or levels of Creation. This has profound implications for life on Earth today, especially our Purpose.

The First phase is the creation of the planets (heavens and the earth). It is what GOD, through the Word (Jesus), formed in the beginning i.e., before Genesis 1. 1.

The second phase was the period of 'now' as referred to in Genesis 1 vs. 2. This again, is an event that predates the Bible. It was a period of lull in creation when it seemed that GOD had forgotten about HIS intention. It was a period of void, emptiness, formlessness, and darkness. The Night time of the creation when the Spirit of GOD hovered over the deep. It was the period of GOD Spirit's creation.

No one knows exactly, how long the Earth was empty and dark and why the Spirit of GOD would be hovering over it. The way the Bible described the Earth is similar to what you would see on other planets: lonely, deserted, dark, rugged, lifeless, unwelcoming, and so on, yet the Spirit of GOD left the throne of GOD and was living under these conditions. Only GOD knows for how many years and why.

GOD wouldn't have allowed His Spirit to leave His present for one second without a purpose let alone for a period that could have easily been a billion of our years. I sincerely believe that the Spirit of GOD was programming or saturating the earth with the various lives that Jesus, the Word would later bring forth in the third level.

The third phase is where Genesis 1 started its account of creation; where GOD called things that were already existing (seeded by the brooding Spirit in the second phase of creation) to show forth Gen. 1: 3 – 25.

The fourth phase was the creation of Man. We shall talk more about this later.

And **the last phase** is the one we are doing now. GOD commanded us and the command was passed down through Adam to us to Dress and Keep the Garden. We don't have the power to create anything new but we can sequence traits, genes, and explore organic and inorganic structure and their characteristics, to make something different from what we have. We're not challenging GOD but demonstrating the god in us.

The world is shifting to climate-friendly energy sources.

Just like we discovered the uses of crude oil in powering our socio-economic life about 200 years ago, we're just getting to know the usefulness of minerals like Lithium, Cobalt, Nickel, and so on.

The truth is that these minerals had been there, latent through Megaannum or Aeon. They didn't just appear today; they had existed since the Second phase of creation.

A deep introspection would show that, we, including our so-called 'discovery', our system of government, our education and scientific breakthroughs, and every aspect of our life had been pre-programmed, pre-established and handed down to us. GOD foresaw that we'd be having discussions about global warming and climate change and would want to move from fossil fuel to a cleaner energy source, HE already schemed everything out and made you and I, the facilitators of these changes and advancements and by so doing, establish HIS kingdom here on earth Phil. 2: 13.

Our so-called discovery is just, we, living out our life as pre-destined for us Eccl. 3: 11.

"Everything is determined, every beginning and ending, by force over which we have no control. It is determined for the insect, as well as for the star. Human beings, vegetables or cosmic dust, we all dance to a mysterious tune, intoned in the distance by an inviable piper."

Albert Einstein

'You Are Not Needy; You Are Needed'

If you were GOD: you just created your biggest project

yet, the earth was your grandest work that took you an uncountable number of years to conceive and execute; what manner of person would you employ to manage the project for you?

Do you know that nobody was found worthy of that role, not in Heaven (the kingdom of GOD)?
As glorious as Lucifer was, as angelic the Angels are, as beautiful, obedient and glorious the Elders in Heaven are, none had the right credentials to man GOD's newest and grandest project which is the earth except you. Incredible, isn't it?

You are found worthy not because of your credentials but because of your make-up. You are the perfect blend of Jesus, the Holy Spirit and GOD HIMSELF because you are a creation of the Word (Jesus Christ), formed from the earth which the Spirit of GOD had impregnated and came alive with the breath from GOD. You are not just human 'meat', you are a human 'being', a vessel that has Jesus, GOD and His Spirit rolled up in one.

I am not psyching you up, this is how the Bible sees you. There must be a compelling reason for GOD to fashion and breathe HIS breath into you instead of calling the earth to produce you as HE did when creating monkeys, Lion, Giraffe, Chimpanzee, trees, and other living things; Do you see GOD going to that extent, for nothing?

You are not needy, you are needed. You are needed here on earth not just to have dominion over the cattle of the field, over the fish in the ocean, over the animals in the wild, over everything that had been created; but more importantly, you're needed to birth to physical what is already seeded in your garden (the spiritual). The treasure you carry in your garden of Eden in form of ideas, inspirations, dreams and insights is not yours but GOD's. It is so important to HIM that HE hid it deep within you from the sight of Satan.

GOD has invested so much into this earth as to watch it fail. That is why HE needs you. HE is ready to do anything within HIS power to back you up if you are committed to launching into the deep within, to ferret out what HE's made you for.

When you examine the lives of the most influential people who
have ever walked among us, you will discover one thread that winds
through them all. They have aligned first with their Spiritual
nature and only then with their physical selves.

Albert Einstein

SIMPLY SPECIAL

*I*n creating plants and animals, GOD simply called the earth, the sea, and the sky. to bring forth what HIS Spirit had incubated in them while the Spirit was brooding over the deep, Gen. 1 from verse 2 to 25. But for Man, GOD came down to the earth, rolled up his sleeve, and got His hand dirty in the mud.

There is something behind that move.

It was easy for GOD to tell the Earth to produce man but HE chose a more laborious way to create man.

GOD wanted to make man to specification, tailor-made for the roles to be assigned in the garden. The same applies to Eve, GOD made her from Adam's ribs - part of Adam to be part of Adam – so that she'd be well-suited for the role of Adam's helper.

GOD couldn't

The earth, the sea and the sky can only mass produce. There's no way the earth would've produce the unique you thus GOD had to step in to produce the unique you.

ask the earth to bring forth man because it was impossible for the earth to produce man with diverse and unique purposes and talents as GOD would have done with HIS personal touch. That is why GOD fashions every one of us by Himself. You're made to order.

7 Elements of Destiny Fulfilment

According to the Bible; these 7 elements must be present in the life of anyone who would fulfill destiny.

They are Adam, Eve, the Garden, Eden, the Serpent, The Tree, and Dominion.

You must be able to bring them together in proper balance and alignment before you can achieve destiny otherwise you become destitute.

<u>Adam</u>

The Bible didn't tell us why GOD created other living things but we know for sure that GOD created Adam for dressing and keeping the garden and managing GOD's other creations. Meaning that Adam was a necessity. As long as there exists the garden, Adam is inevitable.

GOD didn't call the earth to produce Man as HE did with the creation of other living things, rather GOD chose to come down, roll up his sleeve, and beckon on the other GOD-heads when creating Man. GOD was not ready to take chances. GOD had clarity of the kind of creation he wanted and the exact ways to make just that. This further corroborates that Man is planned, purposed, and designed for a specific purpose.

We're a Special Vehicle to Birth the Spiritual (Ps. 127: 3)

I was watching the news on TV one day when a lady appeared that she was suing her parents for giving birth to her without her consent and worse still, expecting her to work to sustain her life, the life she didn't bargain for nor agreed to. (*She's blunt and unapologetic; better than our double-faced society that would be quick to put to death or imprison any parent that kills or mistreats their baby and yet, claims that human being is a biological expression. If you and I are the product of our parents' biological expression, then, should it concern the government what parents do to their product?*).

This lady was taking out her frustration on the wrong person.

As she was not consulted before she was given birth, her parents were not consulted either for the kind of baby they would birth. The truth is that her parent cannot explain why it has to be her; why, out of the billions of sperm cells that her father released, it was hers that fertilized her mum's egg.

They're just a willing vehicle that conveys passengers from

the Spiritual realm to this Physical realm. She should sue GOD, not her parent because the probability of conceiving her is less than one in a billion. If there would be any suing here on earth, it should be the parent that should sue her for denying them the privilege of birthing passengers like Marc Zuckerberg, Adele, Lionel Messi, Coco Gauff, Max Verstappen.

Our parents are just like delivery agents who offered their vehicle (body) to GOD when they had intercourse that turned out to be your pregnancy. They didn't choose you and you didn't choose them. GOD chose who goes where based on HIS cosmic plan.

Your birth is not by accident neither is it by your parent's choice; GOD makes the decision Jer. 1: 5, Eph. 1; 4, Ps. 139: 13 - 16.

You are part of GOD's cosmic plan. Your life is a privilege, not a right, it is planned not an accident; that is why you can't waste it.

<u>Eve</u>

"The Lord GOD said, it is not good for a man to be alone. I will make a helper suitable for him." Gen 2: 18.

Adam thought he had the best of life; he thought his life was a symphony of sorts. He had food in abundance, wealth unquantifiable, success, vitality, peace, joy, merriment, breakthroughs, mobility, security and freedom. Adam's life was just perfect and it couldn't have been better: so, he thought but GOD knew better. GOD knew that for Adam to be perfect, he needed Eve by his side.

We don't know for sure if GOD had a discussion with Adam about HIS plan to make a helper for him, but one thing is sure, Adam earned it.

Understand that it wasn't immediately that GOD made Adam that HE made Eve. Some years probably decades have passed before GOD brought Eve to Adam. And Adam, for the first time, had something he'd call his own, something in his name. Adam did not ask for Eve but GOD made Eve for him; meaning, GOD has the best interest of those who commit themselves to their purpose and assignment here on Earth.

Eve came during the time Adam was already working the garden not before. Adam already found purpose.
This now leads me to the question; what's the purpose of Eve?
The Bible was clear on this, Eve's purpose was to be a helper, not a competitor, not another Adam. The purpose of Eve on Earth was to help Adam achieve his purpose. If Adam achieves his purpose, Eve has achieved hers. Eve was saddled with Someone (Adam), not with things (the garden). This is why women are usually soft and emotional while men are muscular and cerebral. These qualities predispose them to their natural roles; neither is weaker but one is tender the other is firmer.

Competition – The Beginning of the Fall

There can't be 2 Adams in a garden, when Eve tried it, when she dreamt for herself, when she invented a future for herself, they both lost it.

The Bible said in verse 6 of Genesis 3 that when the woman saw that the fruit of the tree was good for food and pleasing to the eyes, and also desirable for 'gaining wisdom'. Let me ask you this question: the wisdom she desired to have, is to what end?

After all, they say: what a man can do, why should a woman bother?

What is more wisdom than the one Adam was operating with? Could any greater wisdom than the one that made GOD trusted Adam so much as to hand over HIS greatest invention yet – the earth, and to trust Adam's judgment in naming everything HE made; be found anywhere here on this earth?

Eve was not comfortable being a helper, she wanted to make decisions and rule, Satan sensed this identity crisis in her and effectively explored it.

OR

It could be that Adam felt threatened by the woman's growing popularity in the garden thus, decided to cut her to size.

In the garden, Eve was the go-to among the occupants of the garden. She's the center of attraction, the force that glued the garden together. The mother of all living beings and everyone flocks to her to the jealousy of the original authority. Adam viewed this as an affront to his diminishing authority, he started ostracizing her, relieving her of many responsibilities, and making the poor woman feel unloved, lonely, and unappreciated.

Finally, Eve found solace with the serpent and for the first time in a long while, she felt appreciated again.

OR

It could also be that Adam misclassified Eve. Remember that what GOD created was a helper but what Adam received was a wife. This simple misjudgment and mischaracterization could be the cause of the tension in the garden. Adam, by seeing Eve as a wife instead of first seeing her as a helper before making her his wife totally limited her role in the garden. All Adam saw was someone to make his food, a weaker vessel, not a partner as intended by GOD. So, it is not surprising that Satan slipped into the garden through the woman, Adam underrated.

Whichever side of the concocted story you believe, you are free, but, don't ask me which part of the Bible I found the narrative from.

What GOD did should preach a thousand words today. GOD drove the 2 of them out without prejudice to what either of them wanted or who was at fault here. Divorcing them was not an option. The 2 of them must now find a dream that they both must work on. They must rise or fall together as one.

Eve can be a Man or Woman. It can be your Spouse, your Friend, your Sibling, your Employee. It can be someone living on your street, or someone, thousands of kilometers away. It might be rich or poor. When you go about working the garden, GOD will send your Eve to you.

You're Eve when you've been charged with someone, you're to help that person in his/her purpose; otherwise, you're Adam who is supposed to birth something to reality.

If you are going to go far in fulfilling your destiny, you must allow an atmosphere for collaboration not competition in your garden. Let everyone GOD has put in your life as Eve be glad and welcoming of their roles in your life. Don't let them feel unappreciated because Serpent is lurking somewhere to use them to derail you.

Satan doesn't need to fight you to stop you; he can use those of your garden to stop you.

<u>THE GARDEN</u>

And the LORD God planted a garden eastward in Eden; and there HE put the Man whom HE had formed.

GOD formed Man outside the garden, GOD planted a garden in Eden then brought the Man HE had made into the garden. I like to provoke your reasoning so as to see the real intentions of GOD for you. GOD made Adam here on earth; then probably took him to heaven for onboarding; while doing so, GOD planted a garden. Think about it for a moment. Why did GOD want Adam to work in the Garden instead of, on the field?

Why didn't GOD allow Adam to find out and decide what to do and where to do it by himself? And what is the difference between working the garden and working the soil as Cain did in Gen. 4?

A Garden is an already prepared farm that has everything in proper balance. In the Garden, the seeds had been planted; you only have to weed and tend to the plants to be able to reap the fruit at the right time. In the Garden, you are spoiled of choices and there is no limitation to what you can achieve but your faith.

Like I said in *3 Keys to Riches,* having a dream is not the same as to dream, when you work the garden (having a dream), you are working toward an answer, an end result that is already guaranteed to succeed. Everyone that works in the garden will certainly be fruitful; however, the fruit produced differs according to what was seeded in the beginning 1Cor. 12: 6.

This is unlike someone working the soil, the fruit that would be produced is certain as you can't plant corn and expect to reap rice. Yes, the fruit to bear is certain but it is not certain if the person would bear fruit at all. While there's a ceiling to what the person working the soil cannot go beyond; there's a barest minimum that the person working the garden cannot go below. You have a garden also; however, it is a Spiritual one. Your garden is that treasure in your heart. The package GOD sent us into this world with. There's no denying the fact that finding your garden takes time and conscious effort. You don't stroll into GOD's Purpose. Adam had it easy but you've to think, seek, pray, examine and explore before you can find your garden Gen. 3: 23, Mt. 7:14.

Be sure of one thing, it is only when you find it that your efforts begin to make meaning. The attendant success far outweighs the efforts you put into finding it. You can achieve in one year what would've naturally taken you ten years to achieve. You've an advantage over competition because it's part of you. You're doing the thing you're naturally made to do; you achieve results faster and cheaper. And more importantly, you are welcomed to HIS kingdom in HIS warm embrace when you die.

If you don't work on your garden, you'd not only have it rough here on earth; but, how do you, in good conscience, expect GOD to open HIS arm to welcome you when you were rebellious and disobedience to the reason, HE sent you to this Earth in the first instance? Were you not sent to this earth for a purpose? How would you give account for your sojourn on this earth?

You carry your purpose inside of you that you must birth into reality. Remember, *you are in this world but not of this world*. You're sent from heaven for a purpose; don't try to be who you're not.

<u>Eden - (Location)</u>

GOD doesn't create anyone without creating a place for that person. Until GOD had planted a garden east of Eden, GOD was not done creating Adam and it wasn't until GOD created him that GOD allowed rain to fall on earth. The implication is that for every one of us alive today, there is what to do (Purpose) and where to do it (People) and by extension, there can't be a problem without man to solve it.

Among the uncountable planets we have, GOD deliberately chose this planet we call the earth. HE made water to gather in a place, HE made atmosphere, HE made the Ozone layer, HE made vegetation and made sure life exists. Our Earth is just perfect for life and this is not by accidence. GOD deliberately made it so.

The specificity did not stop there. GOD deliberately chose a specific place in the east, in a place called Eden; GOD planted the Garden where Adam had everything, he needed to have dominion. Despite the fact that GOD created and owns the expanse of the whole earth, GOD chose a specific place for Adam. Adam needed no reason to maraud through the face of the earth to find definition. GOD had already defined him. Adam didn't have to be a fugitive, he didn't have to be a vagabond, his place was already defined by GOD and it was in Eden; there Adam had his Purpose and assignment stationed.

Don't underestimate the place of Location in your drive to self-discovery. You cannot find your garden until you locate your Eden, that is why it was called the Garden of Eden. You are sent to specific people. Your Location gives meaning to your Purpose. You cannot have dominion if you don't have a domain. There can't be a king without kingdom (king's-domain). GOD that gives you Purpose, has also given you a Place.

<u>East of the Garden – What you can do (usefulness)</u>

For every garden of Eden there's what lies East of the Garden. This world is full of people who are defined by what they can do as against what they should do. Never you confuse what you can do with what you should do. Usefulness is not the same as Purpose.

We didn't think much about what was at the other side of the Garden until GOD drove Adam and Eve out.

At the East of the Garden, Cain worked the ground and we saw the result.

How many of us are working the ground today instead of working the garden? How many of us do whatever our hands find to do? How many have lost their domain in search of what to eat, drink, and wear? Matt. 6: 25 – 33 is as relevant then as it is today. The kingdom of GOD is not meet but power to become what GOD has made you and I to be. The more people living out the treasure in their heart; the more the kingdom of this world is becoming the kingdom of our GOD.

Look at the diagram on the next page: what can you make of it?

Can you see how men choose their level in life with their decisions? We shall take a closer look at the diagram later.

DILIGENCE

Low	High		
Child	King	Purpose	DEDICATION
Masses (Mere Man)	Noble	Usefulness	

In the garden, Adam didn't have to plant; but to discover what GOD already planted by working it out. This qualified Adam to be the friend of GOD. With that, Adam enjoyed everyday visit of the heavenly. GOD came down to fellowship with Adam not because Adam offered any sacrifices, not that Adam gave any worship or any special prayers; as long as Adam kept working the garden, GOD kept coming. Adam ruled as the king when he dedicated himself to his Purpose and was very diligent in it.

Cain didn't have garden to work on, but had to work the soil meaning he had to plant, had to depend on what and who he knows, his trainings, his family background, his environment etc.

Outside Garden, it is dog eats dog. It is about competition in which the winner takes it all and the loser is subjugated and deprived. Cain killed his brother and he'd also have been killed because that is the order that rules. Outside the garden, you're either a villain or a victim. You cannot be outside what GOD has called you into and not be involved in shady deals to stay afloat.

Some people like Adam are rich righteously. They don't have to steal, kill like Cain, enslave like Nimrod. They don't have to sow a seed but their life is so beautiful, so colourful and so fruitful because they work out the seeds GOD had planted in them. They understand that it is not about what they can do that attracts the maximum benefits but what they are made for. They know that: if it is what they can do(usefulness) others will do better, and their reward will be low. They work smart, not hard.

Cain started from scratch. He had to source for the seeds to plant, and he had to sow the seeds in the right field after preparing the ground. Upon the labourious work Cain put in, his harvest was disappointing.

There are more Cains we have today than Adams. The Cains of this world stress usability over purpose. They want to be seen doing something, they don't care if they are moving backward or sidewards, as long as there is motion, as long as they are seen doing something, purpose is tertiary to them.

Imagination Vs Exploration

You can only find purpose when you explore what is inside of you. Knowing the will of GOD for your life is like digging through the earth. At the surface, you encounter topsoil. When you dig further, you encounter rocks, then another layer of soil, then water, then rock. You continue digging you will dig through to the trove of treasure hidden deep within you.

The person that explores and the one that imagines, do similar things but to varying extent - they both think. While the one that explores tarry in the act of soul-searching because s/he would not settle for anything that comes his/her way that is less than what the geological survey (his Purpose) reveals; s/he is intentional. The one that imagines is not intentional. S/he accepts the first thing that interests him/her. Some of them stop at the level of the topsoil, and some stop at the encounter of the first level of rock (challenge). To some, immediately they can dig through the rock, whatever they find is their settlement.

Living in the imagination is like living within the confine of your reach. You work on the seeds your father hands down to you or the seeds you bought from the market or the seeds you saved from the past harvest. You are constantly revolving around the same centripetal, how it has always been done, or how you're trained. Your life is monotonous and boring.

When you explore, you are limitless. You are refreshed every day because a new day brings new opportunities. You are not only growing richer but doing so righteously. You enjoy what you do and you could have done it for free. It is like seeking the kingdom of GOD and his righteousness, then riches, health, influence, power, respect, strength, etc., being added.

Understand that the dominion Adam enjoyed, was over his territory - the garden. Outside of the garden, there is ungoverned space that was ruled by chaos. Adam would have had to fight and struggle with giants, hunters and others; like Cain Gen. 4 vs 14. But inside of your garden, you are at an advantage over any competition; it is your garden, your territory. If properly fortified and guarded, even the serpent cannot slip through inside.

How to Know Which Location Is Best for You

You're a chosen generation. You're not like any other, everything about you including your 'office' and location had been predefined.

Before you can talk of having dominion, you must first have a domain. No king is truly a king without a kingdom. GOD had defined your territory over which you exercise your power and authority. If there's no defined territory, there'd always be struggle and attrition; GOD is not the author of confusion.

To whom you're sent is also as important as the message is. The location of your Purpose is so important that they call it the 'Garden' of 'Eden'. Don't be fooled that you can sow your seed anywhere. If Satan cannot stop you from sowing your seed, he will try that you sow it in the wrong places Matt. 13: 4 - 8.

So, how do you know the right place for your seed, the best location for your office, where your garden is located?

1. Your Location Doesn't Have to Be Your State of Origin or Place of Birth

The first thing to know is that your garden may not be where you were born.

Judging by the sheer number of people who discover their purpose outside of where they were born, their state or country of origin, both in the Bible and in this present age, it'll be unwise to reject considering jetting out of their locality to fulfill their destiny.

Gen. 2:8 told us that: God planted a garden eastward in Eden, and there he put the Man whom HE had formed. Ask yourself, why didn't GOD form Adam from the same place HE planted the garden? If you don't understand me, why was Adam born in the West but his purpose lies in the East?

God told Abram to get out of his locality, his comfort zone, to a place where his purpose was Gen. 12: 1. GOD was so particular about location that when Abram went beyond the place in Gen. 12: 8, GOD stopped speaking to him Not until Abram returned to the place and was separated from Lot that GOD spoke again in Gen. 13: 14.

Aside Adam and Abraham that had the location of their purpose outside of where they were born; Jacob, for 80years in the land of his nativity, didn't amount to anything. But just 20 years in one obscure place called Padana'ram, Jacob achieved in 20years what he couldn't achieve in 80years.

The same incident played out in the life of Moses, Joseph, Paul, and more importantly, our Lord Jesus Christ. Nobody would have heard of the name Daniel, Shadrach, Meshack, and Abednego if they had remained in Israel.

I can't conclusively tell you that your allocation is not your locality, however, it is a sign of abdication of responsibility to assume that you are sent to the people you grew up with or that you can make it anywhere.

When you look at some of those working out their Purpose today, they became so after moving from where they were born. Elon Musk, Bill Gates, Jeff Bezos, Albeit Einstein, Anthony Joshua, Tony Elumelu, Aliko Dangote, Lionel Messi, Cristiano Ronaldo.

Some people stayed in the same environment for 20, 30, or 40 years still counting without amounting to anything. The place they currently occupy is a rented apartment they were born in, the same place their father lived until he died, they have continued that terrible path.

Look at your life, is your life refreshing or stagnant?

Sometimes, it is not prayer that you need. You just need to be intentional to break that terrible cycle in your family. You just need to take a discomforting step like Jacob. GOD never told Jacob to get out of Canaan but situation pushed him. Change your environment when things have remained the same with you. GOD may tell you where your location is, like Abraham, but, sometimes, GOD would lead you.

Another approach might be GOD using situation to drive you as HE did to Jacob, Joseph, and Daniel. Another way might be you are rejected like in the case of Jesus Christ. You might be too big for the same environment as the sons of the prophet in 2 Kg 6.

GOD can also ask you to stay in the place of your nativity if there is a subsisting promise that is location-based like in the case of Isaac and the Apostle before they received the Holy Spirit. The approach is endless but I must point out that moving out of your location because of famine or economic situation has never yielded any positive result. Take for example: Abraham, who nearly lost his life while running away from famine. Isaac stayed back in the land and despite the ongoing famine, he prospered. Naomi ran away from Israel because of famine but returned almost empty. It is only beggars who left their country because of famine and returned with loads of riches.

You don't change your location because of economic situation except you're an economic leper.

2. Your Location Brings Out the Best in You.

Everyone knows that no matter how rich, well-maintained, and diverse a garden could be, the garden would not bring out anything without water. Water acts as the force carrier, the enforcer or expressor of the potential of the garden. Without water, the Garden remains sterile and unproductive.

Water gives vim to the innate life in the garden.

Take note of Gen. 2: 10. A river from Eden water the garden. When the River flows into the garden, the embedded seeds that had hitherto been innate and hidden would spring forth and germinate. This is the purpose of the river.

As the river signifies the best location for Adam, your place is where ideas come to you.

Don't look for a developed place, don't be moved by traffic but where the idea comes to you most. The more ideas that flood into you, the closer you are to where GOD has planted for you.

What so many people do is that they want to marry 2 opposing realities together. They were in a place where ideas flowed like a river but because the place was yet a garden, they shipped themselves to a boisterous city. They find themselves out of their element, they have to shape in to blend with their out-vironment at the expense of being at home with their in-vironment. When you are out of radius, clashes erupt between who you are and who you are becoming.

Understand yourself first. *The river that brings life to a garden can also cause erosion to another.* Your natural environment would empower you to fulfill your destiny.

3. You See Problem, You See Opportunity.

You have been told to look out for opportunities. Opportunity looks more like a challenge, a problem, or an inconvenience initially until you decide to see through it.

The reason why GOD didn't allow rain to fall on earth was because there was no man to work the ground Gen. 2: 5 & 6. Where you see shrubs, weeds, where you see problems, know that the solution is already existing.

Problems are not there to stop you but as a rite of passage to your immortality.

You will never see a problem that you are not part of its solution. You are either a direct or an indirect solution. You're either a part or a final solution to the problem in the community that GOD has put you. No one is useless in the problem that is ravaging his/her community.

When a problem lasts generations; know that the people are the problem.

Gideon, unlike others in his time, saw the problem but didn't accept it as normal. He would not be forced to live in caves like animals as others Jdgs. 6 & 7. While others were hiding in caves, Gideon was grinding wheat in the winepress.

How can someone be grinding a dry wheat in a wet area?

This shows the kind of person Gideon was. A go-getter. This is why the Angel addressed him as a 'mighty warrior'.

Gideon, just by standing up to do something different from what the people had always done, 32000 men stood by him. You don't know what influence you can wade until you stand.

One of the many lies Satan would tell you to dissuade you from the Purpose of GOD for you is by asking you if you are the only one. Satan would ask you, what happens to others or why are they not doing something about the problem? Satan may even tell you that you don't have what it takes, or tell you to leave and run away from that place.

You may not be the direct solution to that problem but down the line, you're strongly engraved in the solution. It means, if that your part, which you think is inconsequential, is not there, the problem will not be solved conclusively.

There were times when Israel lacked men to fight war. They had to depend on singing. Had the singers said they were singers, not soldiers, so, don't have any duty on the battlefield; Israel would have lost the battle.

What I am saying is that when you see general problem in your locality, it is not best to run away thinking you are not the specific solution. You may not be the direct solution in the war like soldiers are, but you may be an indirect solution like singers.

4. Your Location Gives unto You Not Just Take from You.

The river flows from Eden into the Garden to water the garden. Where you give and you don't receive in return, that environment might not be yours. If you look around and you are the only person doing well in any environment; you may need to relocate to where you will be nourished and be strengthened.

A lone tree would soon be uprooted by any wind.

A tree provides shades and fruits from the nourishment provided by the same environment. Don't be blackmailed emotionally into staying in an environment that would not bring out the best in you.

As it is possible to be in an environment that doesn't add to you, you should also do not settle in an environment that you cannot add anything to. Don't be a misfit in any environment because, it is better to give only than to always receive only but it is best to be where you give and receive in good measure Lk. 6: 38.

5. Your Effort Is Magnified; You Achieve Results Effortlessly.

To show that Adam was at the right place, despite rain not failing, Adam was effective in achieving results, thanks to the river that flowed into his garden. Isaac wanted to leave his location because of famine, but GOD told him to remain there. Despite everyone in the environment failing and becoming frustrated, Isaac increased 100fold to the point that they accused him of using juju.

When you are at your allocated space, the prevailing circumstance in your environment doesn't determine your experience. When others are experiencing a casting down, you'll be experiencing lifting. This is also a testament that people struggle when they are out of sync not only with their purpose but also with the environment. It's only in your allocated place, that greatness would locate you.

6. You're Sure, That Your Future Is Guaranteed There.

The above-discussed ways are not cast in stone. They are to guide you. One thing you must realize is that, sometimes, your location might not look like where you'd want to settle in, it might fail all of the above 5 tests; yet, GOD is telling you to stay.

GOD led Abraham from Haran (present-day Turkey), where he had acquired much wealth and also influence, to one remote place called Canaan. A place where nothing was working, no access to the sea, no access to the market, nothing. To make matters worse, famine there was a regular occurrence.

If it were you, would you stay in such a place?

Isaac faced a similar situation only that unlike Abraham, Isaac's horizon wasn't that broad. He had not traveled outside of there, so, this was his own mecca of sorts, his own Hong Kong, Singapore, Seoul, Tokyo, New York, London, or Shanghai.

Despite never being away from Canaan, he too desperately wanted to leave because of the prevailing socio-economic situation of the land. Up till now, I have not understood why it was only in Canaan that famine was so common that in less than 50 years, there's at least 2 famine occurrences and yet, just about 100km away, in Egypt, there was flourishing. Canaan looked accursed, Yet, GOD told him to stay.

Doing as GOD bade him, Isaac grew up to become the most successful person in that land.

The event surrounding Pentecost is arguably the most fascinating story whose implications bear more impact than being expounded. From where JESUS departed from to Jerusalem, it was a 7day journey. What was so special about Jerusalem that JESUS told the disciples to wait there until they received the gift of the HolyGhost Lk. 24: 49?

The answer is found in Acts 2: 5. GOD wanted to give the Jews another opportunity to receive JESUS and HIS Messiahship. It was planned that renowned Jews all over the world would gather in Jerusalem at that time so that every one of them would hear directly from GOD not from a prophet. This is when GOD undid what HE did in Genesis 11. Men now speak of the wonderful works of GOD instead of their own work.

You don't know what GOD has planned out to accomplish, but when you stay at GOD's apportioned place for you, you will be the ladder that reaches from this earth to heaven.

When GOD says stay, it is because that place has the right conditioning for the next thing HE wants to do for you.

GOD may explicitly tell you to stay or HE may make you feel strongly about the place. This feeling is not about being emotional, it is not about the fear of the unknown, it is not about having a deep connection or the memory the place conveys. You don't know why; you just feel like you want to stay back. At this moment, you will not know for how long or what you are staying back for, but there's such a strong urge for you to stay. Maybe after obeying the gut feeling, the reason and the duration would be crystallized. Sometimes, you choose a place not because of what it has to offer now but because you know deep down within you that the area will bring you good fortune soon.

Satan would have come around in those moments to dislodge the disciples from Jerusalem. He'd have told them that they should be able to receive the gift of the HolySpirit anywhere in this world. Never fall for Satan's trickery; if you don't know the plan of GOD for you, Satan knows it, and he plans to scuttle it.

7. You are closer to GOD there.

When Adam was in the garden, he was face-to-face with GOD. Outside the garden, Adam and his children had to offer special sacrifices to seek GOD's face.

When you constantly feel exposed, when the thought of death, loss, or shame is your everyday companion when you're anxious and agitated in your soul and you always fear the worst.

Then you're not at the right location.

If it is the opposite. If you are not afraid of any exigency not because of your savings or the people you know, then you might be rightly located.

OR

When your Spiritual energy is constantly being drained for no obvious reason, it means that you're not at your allocated place. Your Spiritual energy is being drained because you're dissipating energy doing what should naturally be GOD's role. You have orphaned yourself from GOD, therefore, you have to fend for yourself. When you're anxious and always in constant fear, you're not at the right place Gen. 12: 12.

OR

When you don't feel GOD is near or your spiritual barometer is critically low, check yourself if you are at the right place.

OR

When you have to struggle for everything you have, you may be wrongly be positioned.

How Location Not Effort Might Determine Your Life

One very important lesson from the parable of the sower is how location determines the destiny of men. The sower that sowed by the wayside, the one that sowed on the rock, together with the one that sowed among thorns, all ended up the same-poor, broke and destitute despite making similar efforts as the one that sowed on the good land.

You see people petered out trying to turn a desert into a garden. You see people underachieving, intelligent people scrapping by, hardworking fellows struggling financially, and you blame it on the spiritual force.

Sometimes it is not a spiritual attack but a wrong location. GOD told the children of Israel in Jeremiah 4 to break their fallow ground and not to sow among thorns. GOD said so because it is important. It is not only your efforts that bring the result, the location also matters.

In what ways are you sowing among thorns? Is your environment magnifying your efforts or killing it?

We, like plant; that we share similar characteristics or purposes does not mean we would share the same requirements for growth. Ask any farmer.

Rice and Cassava both need water but planting Cassava in the place where you should plant Rice would result into massive lost. White melon seed looks like Sesame seed and they are both used similarly, yet, they don't grow well in the same environment. Maize and peanuts are both grains but the optimal condition for both are not the same.

That we're colleagues, friends, mentors, and so on, does not mean we would do well in the same location. Everyone is unique with unique environmental needs to fruit optimally. Don't assume, ensure. Eccl. 10: 15.

<u>**The Serpent (Friend-enemies)**</u>

Do you know that Satan is not GOD's adversary, but yours? Not quite sure?

Ask yourself these questions: Is Satan the accuser of GOD? Can Satan deceive GOD? The answer is no. Satan recognizes GOD and pays obeisance to GOD, Job 1: 6, Zec. 3: 1 – 5, Rev. 12: 10. You may be surprised, but Satan's agelong ambition is to have this earth to himself and he sees you and I as the usurper; trying daily, making case before GOD that human beings should be destroyed.

Have you ever given it a thought that there were 2 trees GOD asked Man not to eat from and the 2 of them were in the middle of the garden meaning they were close to each other Genesis 2: 9b. One tree would supposedly made them live forever and the other would give them wisdom. Satan convinced them to eat from the Tree of Knowledge but not from the Tree of Life. Why was Satan interested in Man being wise when he knew that God would kill them? Of what use is wisdom in the grave?

Satan would always pretend to have your best interest at heart, he'd advise you to do nothing, sit by, or do it grudgingly. He would try fronting self-preservation as the reason why you'd accept the status quo. He will make you hate, make you envy, make you take offense.

Anytime you are vengeful, anytime you want to prove a point, anytime you fear, hate, or jealous, look at the other side, just know that Satan has you where he wants you. Satan is never your friend; he is only interested in dispossessing you of your glory. Satan played Adam and he is using the same trick on you.

<u>The Trees</u>

The Garden of Eden is Adam's. GOD gave it to him to keep and dress it. At the middle of the same garden, GOD planted 2 trees which Adam must not eat from. Adam would work under the tree; Adam would trim and prune it; birds would perch on the trees; goat could eat from the leaf but the real keeper of the garden could not eat from it no matter what. To make it more tempting, the trees are right in the middle of the garden. Imagine waking up in the morning and the tree is the first to greet Mr. Adam: 'Good morning, Mr. Adam, blessed of the Lord; look, while you were sleeping, I bear this beautiful and sumptuous berry, grape, apple; you can make the best wine with it or you can make a quick smoothie or just juice it'.

If you can resist that urge, then you are in the top 0.0001% of human. It means that you'd have no problem keeping 100% of your resolutions; you are just too perfect.

Is the tree a temptation or a training?

Paul said that everything is lawful but not everything is expedient 1 Cor. 6: 12. He said further that he had learned to keep his body under check so that he would not miss heaven 1 Cor. 9: 27.

The mentality of a purposeful person is to have it at the back of the mind that not all things are permissible. That others are doing it, does not make it ok for him to do it. The Bible said that Daniel purposed in his heart that he would not defile himself with the king's meal, understand that it wasn't only Daniel and the 3 Hebrew boys that were Jews in the king's palace then Dan. 1: 3 and 6. That is the foundation that, made him relevant over the span of 70 years under 4 to 5 different reigns and kingdoms.

If you want to live out your purpose on Earth, you must make certain inconveniencing personal decisions. It is a kind of sacrifice that shows that you can be trusted.

Imagine a glutton as the president of your nation; imagine someone who cannot control the sexual urge as a Pastor.

Samson was one such person. Saul was made king but he was so insecure and always wanting validation from the people.

Satan's advice in Matt. 4: 6, seemed biblical, but JESUS refused because, to HIM, it is not about the basic, HE made the decision not to do anything that does not glorify GOD.

In HIS Image and Likeness

The Image and Likeness that we share with GOD is not

just the physical attribute nor is it mental or emotional but the unfathomableness of our soul. GOD told the other Godheads that, for the kind of responsibility we're expecting the Man we are creating to shoulder, the Man must be as unlimited as we are.

From whom much is expected of, much should be given.

There's nothing GOD can do, that we cannot do. Does this sound outlandish? Yes, it does, even to me. If not that the Bible said so in Gen. 11: 6, Jn 14:12, Ps. 82: 6, Jn 10: 34, I would have slapped myself back to 'life'.

HUMILITY, the KEY to unlocking the 99.999% of You

Look at the diagram below, you can see that our earlier claim is not preposterous. It is not totally out of place to claim that You and I are the small version of GOD.

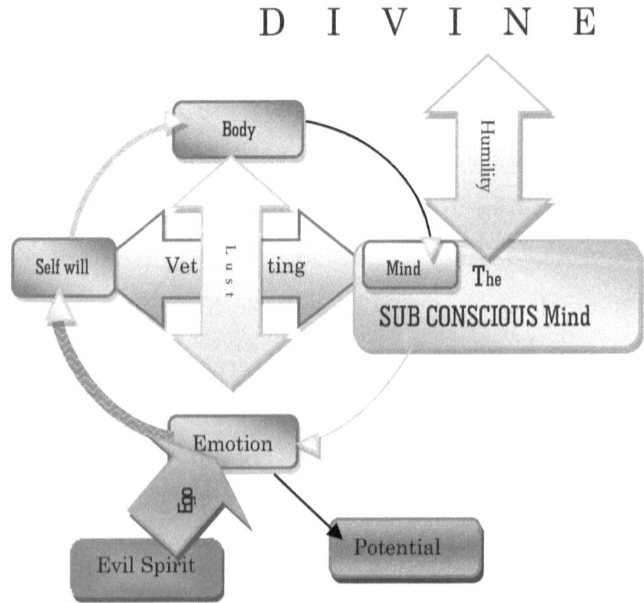

We are connected to the boundless wisdom, possibility, and power in the Spirit if our humility is so strong enough to withstand it, Matt. 5: 5, 1Pet. 5: 5, James 4: 6.

The Human Spirit can connect to the Divine when that person is humble like a child by believing whatever the father said concerning him/her and acting accordingly Matt. 19: 14.
Look at Moses, he was described as the meekest man on earth; look at how he dealt with the gods of Egypt. Moses so confused them that they joined Moses in hurting their people Ex. 8: 7.
When we talk about Humility, we are not referring to ingratiating yourself with fellow human beings (that may be idolatrous) but, we are talking about you believing in GOD to the point of 'would rather lose everything than lose my faith in GOD'. You're not humble until your self-preservation, ego, desire, interest, and every self are subsumed and subjected to GOD's word.

The reason many people (including myself), may never reach 99.999% of our potential is because, of the limitation of trying to belong, has imposed on us. The social conditioning, the fear of failure, the fear of disappointment and rejection, the desire to blend in, not to upset the status quo, to belong (pride), and so on, have 'promoted' man far below our godlike make-up.

If you have not performed the act of turning an ordinary rod into a snake that swallows other snakes without increasing in size, then you have not reached 10% of your potential. If you have not told a mountain to be suspended in the air and be cast into the sea, you are still operating below capacity. Until you can part the sea, tell time to stay still, and bring down clouds as pillars of fire and of light, you've not yet reached 50% of your capacity.

That which travels faster than the speed of light

If you are still having a hard time believing in your great and almost unlimited potential, consider the fastest Man-made object yet, the NASA Solar Probe. It can travel at almost 700000km/hr., meaning it can travel from one end of the earth to the other end in just a little over one minute.

This astonishing and body-crushing speed of this man-made object is nothing compared to the least of GOD's capabilities which is the Speed of Light. The Speed of light travels at over 1 billion km/hr. Imagine the insane speed of 1 billion kilometers per hour. The fastest fighter jet in the world today is just 3661km/hr. meaning it will take our best fighter jet 33 years to do what the speed of light would do in an hour.

What if I told you that you have something faster than the speed of light? That thing is right within you.

It is the Speed of Mind.

It is so fast that it is impossible to fathom how fast it is. Your thought is faster than the speed of light. Where the speed of light will take years to get to, your thought would get there in a second.

Isn't that amazing?

To put it in proper perspective, your mind can travel this fast because it is a Spirit. The impossibility that exists in the world doesn't affect what you can do if only you flow in the frequency of the heavenly John 3: 8.

How deep is your soul?

There is a tale about one young man who lived over 2000 years ago. This young man was rejected, ostracized, and uncatered for because he was sick. His sickness drove him away from people and civilization, and he chose the dead as his companion.

Legend has it that he was so feared and fierce that the whole community could not dare cross his path. The young man was so famous that he was named after the city, the Gerasene's man in Mathew 8 from verse 28.

You know the story, right? Yes, you do.

But what, you and many people don't know about the story is how possible for a man to carry a load for years, that over 2000 heavily fed swine could not carry for a second.

You are more than what people around you can see. You are eternal, unlimited, and borderless. The depth of your soul is unfathomable. Limiting yourself to your physical and visible part is unwise. My Bible told me that, after GOD breathed into the man HE had formed, Man became a living soul.

This particular act is what separates us from other animals, the breath of GOD in us. The breath is not to give us life (other animals have life in them) but to make us a living soul or being.

What does it mean to be a living soul?

Like I said in '3 Keys to Riches' the Soul is a vessel, a container. It is that part of us that resembles GOD. The bottomless, the endless part of us.

This is why there is no limit to what you can achieve. As long as it is in your heart (within your garden), you can attain it.

We are on a MISSION here on Earth

It is hypocritical to confess you have faith in GOD and at the same time you are not living out your purpose. This is akin to saying that you are a product of biological expression. You are agreeing to it that GOD didn't create you at all, but you became, by the desire of your parents.

I don't know which will be more tolerable between those who say there is no GOD and those who say GOD is stupid for creating them for no particular reason.

What if Heaven is like this?

I remembered when I was a kid, I remembered when my father sent me to buy him something at a neighbourhood market. I would go about singing the things he had asked me to buy until I reached where the thing was being sold. I dared not play or do any other thing that might make me forget what that thing is.

There was a day he sent me to buy garri to make eba as lunch for the whole family. On my way, I came across a man who was walking with a life leopard (If you lived in the Ebute-Metta area of Lagos around that time, you would have seen this man. This man would cut himself with the knife but the knife wouldn't hurt him. the man was a magician who performed many tricks that held everyone spellbound). This is how I stayed and watched the man perform for about an hour before I got myself back to the message my dad had sent me. It was then it dawned on me that I had forgotten what he sent me. Fearing going home empty-handed, I bought what he usually sent me: paracetamol and vitamin c.

That day, eehn, I thought I would die. The kind of beating I received, the mark is still on me till today. I don't know if it was because I kept the family hungered for over an hour, or if it was all the money in the house that I wasted, but deep within me, I knew I deserved every stroke of the cane.

After that incident, my dad now devised another approach, each time he sent something, he would write it out for me on a piece of paper. Believe me, this saved me a lot of hassle. On countless occasions, I would go to a chemist shop when I was supposed to go to mummy Sikirat which sells foodstuff, sometimes, I would go to mummy Sikirat when I was supposed to go to mummy Daniel which sells drinks. Each time I went to the wrong shop, instead of *buying what they sold, they would direct me to the right place to buy what I was sent.*

You know my story; but do you know this is what is going on, in the lives of so many people and maybe, in your life also? Sadly, unlike me, you don't have the liberty to have a second chance to make things right after you have returned to your father with the message. What do you think would happen if you return to heaven with no result to show for GOD's investment in you for the task, HE commissioned you for? What would you tell HIM when HE asked you, 'Where is the thing I asked you to buy with the Talent I gave to you'?

Don't be too carried away by this world's activities that you forget to live out the reason for your living.

You're not an accident, you are not willed according to flesh but according to the will of your heavenly father who hath called you out of darkness, out of groping, out of your imagination; into HIS marvelous light and Purpose.

CHOOSING YOUR LEVEL

See thou man diligent in his work, he shall stand before kings and not mere men.
Prov 22:29

I have said, Ye are gods; and all of you are children of the most high. 7 But ye shall die like mere

men...psalms 82 vs 6 & 7.

There is a story of a young boy, the only child of a rich man. His father on his dying bed, asked the boy to choose just one thing among his many estates and the rest would go to the maid.

The young boy didn't like it but he had no choice as the father was not going to change his mind.

A day before the final day his father gave him to make the choice, he went to an old sage in his neighbourhood to seek advice. The sage told him to choose the maid. Confused but out of respect for the sage, he did as the sage advised.

He went to the father and told the father that he was choosing the maid.

The father couldn't hide his admiration for his son's choice, sat up from his bed, and said, my son, the reason I permit you to choose only one thing out of my many things, is to make you see how your choice makes or mars you.

You are growing up and very often, you will be making choices. The choice of who to become, what to do, where to go, who to marry, job to take. Every day you will have to choose out of many competing options. The choice you make goes a long way down the tunnel of your life. The choice will decide how you will come out on the other side or if you will come out at all. When you choose, you should always remember that you reject the others. Don't even think you can play the fast one on nature by shying away from making choices when you need to because not making choices is a choice also. You can't have your cake and eat it too. And with your choice comes opportunity costs, the other competing choice, and what they offer.

Many people of your age, will choose my collection of cars. They do this to impress and to feel belong. Showing off on someone else's sweat. A big older version of you will choose my houses and all my landed property because it wants stability and security. Some will go for cash and my stock investments; they want that freedom and mobility. A clever child might go for my company but it

> You chose the maid. Everything the maid has,
> now belongs to you.
> When you choose service over possession, you
> become indispensable and that enthrones you
> over others that choose possession and title.

is only a wise child will choose the maid that has been with me since the beginning.
You choose the maid and everything the maid has now belongs to you. As you can see, it is possible to make just one choice and have everything.

Since you have chosen him, I don't need to advise you much again. You have shown shrewdness and proven to me that you are far better than most people. The only thing I would like to add is that you take care of him and listen to him, never let him depart your side, let him become your father, your guide and he will lead you in the right way. The maid represents service, it represents wisdom and it represents empathy. Let these qualities be your guide in life.

The father fell on the son's lap and gave up the ghost.

The moral of this story is that some choices would give you money but take freedom from you, some other choices would give you freedom but leave you penniless, and with some choices, you can have both. You can become king, you can become noble, you can become mere man; all are the choices you make.

LIVING FOR BREAD ALONE

Deut. 8:3 and Matt 4:4 said that man shall not live by bread alone. Man's needs can be categorized into 2 broad branches:

Live for Bread or Live for the Word.

Everyone knows what bread does. Bread is about having your sustenance and needs being met.

If all, you ever do in your life is to work, to earn a living, live a comfortable life, then you are living for bread. When you are never concerned about how your work is meeting or affecting other people's needs but you are in it for the salary, then you are living for yourself, living for your needs, title, and bread.

When you live for the Word, you are concerned about what GOD says about you. You live for GOD's purpose, you live for potentials, for dreams, for light, for impact, and for service. When your work keeps giving after you have given it out like a living word, it keeps living and changing lives. It doesn't matter where, it doesn't matter if you are recognized or not, it does matter if it is a white, blue, gray, pink, green, gold, open, or no collar job; what matters is that you are doing something beyond your needs. You are using your talent or office to bring to life, GOD's kingdom on earth; you live for the word.

2 Cor 9: 10, says that GOD gives bread to the eater and seed to the sower… You decide which of these you want. Remember, choosing to be **an eater** always leaves you in perpetual need. Yes, GOD may always meet your needs, but you'll always be needy. An eater would go hungry, there is no escape, and worst still no freedom of choice, you are so engrossed in where your next meal would come from that you don't have the time to serve GOD.

An eater would never live for purpose, would never live for impact, all he lives for is his/her needs.

This is not why GOD made you. You are not an animal, you are not a bird that does not sow nor plow, you are made to work out GOD's riches in you, thus you are a Sower, not an eater.

An eater would see a challenge and complain. He blames the government, the rich, the economy, blame everyone else but himself. He has this entitlement mentality and when that's not giving him what he wants, he switches to playing the victim card. He wants everything to be given to him on the platter of gold. He has greatness locked somewhere inside of him because working out that greatness requires dedication, diligence, discipline, and faith, so he would rather remain small than reach for the stars.

A sower is a person who works out the seed (the word of GOD) in his heart. A Sower works out the seeds of GOD and nurtures them to fruitfulness. (3 Keys to Riches).

A sower is not a needy but needed. Sower is the first to partake of the fruit 2 Tim 2: 6. The Sowers are usually in short supply, so they are paid in premium. Another advantage is that Sowers meets eaters' needs therefore, eaters are always surety to Sowers Pro.17:8. JESUS told us not to live our lives as though we're worse than birds of the field; and that we should not allow the fear of what we shall eat, wear, or live stop us from living out our Purpose. HE went on to say that as long as we are going about the Purpose GOD made us for, our needs will always be met.

3 levels of Man; How we seal our fate.

DILIGENCE

Low	High		
Child	King	Purpose	DEDICATION
Masses (Mere Man)	Noble	Usefulness	

Every Man grows up to become any of these: Man, Mere Man, or King, according to Prov 22: 29. The person you become is first your choice, then you act.

Your choice: if you choose to do what you can do or what you should do. When you decide to work your garden or the soil. If it is about what your hand can find or what you are made for. If it is about capability or responsibility, usefulness or purpose. Whose work you dedicate yourself to (yours or GOD's), shows who employs you; and who employs you is who rewards you.

Your act: how much of yourself do you give to that work? If you give much of yourself, you either become a king or a noble; but if you give little of yourself to the work, you become either a mere man or a child, all depends on the choice you made in 1 above.

Dedication plus Diligence puts you in the class of persons you belong to, not GOD, not prayer, not Sacrifice. As much as these things are important, they, on their own, can't make you.

We misinterpret the Prov. 22: 29 by not capturing the whole message thereby missing out on the importance. We only look at the passage from the account of being diligent. We often fail to ask ourselves the question: **diligent in what?**

The passage said, see thou a man diligent in 'his' work.

Meaning that there are two kinds of work: **'his work'**, the one being referred to in Prov. 22; 29. There is a higher and purer level of work, that is **'HIS work'** Gen. 2: 15. Diligence in either earns you a reward, but what reward, is a question of who engages you.

Diligence in 'his' work i.e., what your hand findeth to do Eccl. 9:10, makes you stand before kings as a minister. Being diligent in HIS work (your divine mandate) earns you dominion and authority Genesis 1:26. Being Diligent in GOD's purpose for your life makes you the king that others stand before.

I don't know which reward you want, remember the enormous power, the king's command, and remember that the minister serves at the behest of the king. We have heard of wonderful and dutiful ministers who were hanged (Haman, the king butler, John the Baptist), heaven did not fall. Any war that would consume the king would have consumed many soldiers, the kingdom, and even the ministers first, don't take my word for it, research it yourself.

The question to ask yourself to know which Man you are, is: 'Am I diligent?' and 'diligent in what?'.

Ask yourself: what am doing, is it what I am supposed to be doing or what I decide to do because I can do it?

After GOD had called the Earth to produce after their kinds in Gen. 1: 11 nothing was physically (Gen. 2: 5) not until GOD put Man HE had formed into the garden to work and dress everything to life Gen. 2 vs 15.

From the foregoing, we can safely conclude that; what GOD expected from Adam was to bring to physical what HE had buried in the ground.

It doesn't matter what GOD wants or has made available, without Man in the equation, nothing exists physically. Adam was to nurture and develop GOD's idea. Adam didn't have to plant, Adam didn't have to till the ground, Adam surely didn't have to decide what to do to make himself relevant in the garden, Adam only needed to work on what GOD had implanted.

This, unlike Genesis 4 verse 2: Cain, works the ground. Cain had to decide the meaning of his life. There was no garden for Cain to work out but the soil meaning that Cain had to find definition and purpose by his power and attainment. Whatever Cain would become, he had to do it all by himself because he was out of GOD's plan and purpose.

The original purpose of GOD for us is to work and dress the garden not to work the ground.

Working the ground requires that you decide what seeds to plant, when to plant, and where to plant them; you decide your usefulness by yourself. In working the garden, you don't decide anything but dutifully work out that which has been planted; you dress it as such as to bear fruits.

Whose work are you working on? GOD's own or Man's own.

Forget it, if what you are working on is not GOD's own, you shall have it rough. Don't live your life with Eccl 9 vs. 10 as your motto; it is for those who are dying.

Consider this, Adam worked the garden, and with that,

GOD gave him dominion but Cain worked the soil but ended up being a killer and a vagabond. I am not saying that choosing a career or profession, working for someone else will make you end like Cain. But if you do so when it is not your garden, you have to do a lot more, so that you don't end up using the chunk of your life, changing from one job to another without accompanying anything just as it was with Jacob before Gen 30 vs. 30b.

Who is a king?

Ascension to kingship is by inheritance. Kingship is a natural office that is handed down through lineage meaning that you have to be connected before you can have the chance of becoming the king in the future.

Gal. 4 vs 1 says: '…as long as the heir is a child, he is no different from a slave, although he owns the whole estate.' Roman 8: 16-17, The Spirit himself testifies with our spirit that we are GOD's children. [17] Now if we are children, then we are heirs-heirs of GOD and co-heirs with Christ…'

The would-be King just needs to grow up to ascend to the throne. 'Kings are born not made'.

We are all born with certain advantages for certain possibilities. We are children of GOD, the King of kings, we have blue blood running through our veins. There is no other definition we need than the one our birth in Christ had conferred on us. We are princes and princesses and we shall reign on earth.

How Destiny is Won and Lost.

There was this boy (Adebayo or Bayo for short) born into royal family. He had a close friend (Tayo) who they grew up together before Tayo left the village to the city. Tayo came around one day and decided to see Bayo the Prince. Upon seeing each other, they ran to hug; they were delighted to see after over 15 years apart.

It is natural to expect them to talk about their lives and how things had been with them. Tayo had a lot to share about his new status, his many girlfriends in the city, his comfortable life, his car, his salary, his job, his plan and everything you would expect from someone having a successful life.

Adebayo, the prince, didn't have much to say about his life. Before he could say one thing about himself, he would have said 3 things about his father or the throne. It was as if, he was nothing without the throne and this made him start to detest everything he had lived for all these years.

After they parted, Adebayo became sullen and depressed. He questioned how he had allowed life to pass him by. I can't do anything for myself except my father allowed it. I can't have many girlfriends like my friend Tayo because it is taboo for a king-to-be to be philandering. I can't even work and earn money because of being prepped for the throne.

He looked at his life and for the first time in his life, wished he was not a Prince. He wished he could be free to do what he wanted to do, eat like every other person, be like every other person, and especially, like Tayo. He decided that he had

had enough of this kingship bruhaha.

He went to his father that he was recusing himself from the throne and that the father should give him his share of the property that fell to him.

You see, many people have lost their place in destiny because the throne, GOD is preparing them for; takes a lot of inconveniences and time. They don't like to wait through for it. they see their friends' social façade; they feel life is going by them.

They see people driving cars in their domain forgetting that they would soon be driving in convoy if only they could wait to mount the throne. They hear their mate getting married and having children and they feel left behind. If only they could wait out the process, their friends, their children would serve their children.

As a king-to-be, GOD is interested in every detail of you so that you'd not be an accident waiting to happen. You can't marry anyhow girl, you need Eve. Aside from the normal education that others receive; you also receive special training that may not be convenient but necessary.

People might disappoint you a lot of the time; they sincerely wanted to do as promised, but they're no longer in power nor have the strength anymore; this is not to frustrate you out of your Purpose but rather a boot camp to teach you self-belief and faith in GOD. You might have been thrust into tragedy early in life; it's not to stop you but to give you courage, patience, faith and wisdom.

GOD would not allow you to be tempted beyond what HE has given you the fortitude to bear.

Whatever challenges you faced that is uncommon to your friends and acquittances, don't question the love of your father, don't run away from the crown because of the challenge.

The head that would wear the crown must be shaped to the shape and size of the crown.

You are not Tayo so, you don't have to be.

A Noble, a king without a throne

Being a King or being a noble requires diligence. You have to constantly be better at what you do. While the king has a throne, the noble has office. The king's domain is territorial and bounded, but the noble's domain is knowledge and without physical boundary. A wise king would guard and develop his territory, and a wise noble would guide and deepen his knowledge.

One major distinguishing factor of a King from a Noble aside from the throne is the method of becoming; kingship is by inheritance; nobility is by acquirement.

As a noble, you have a price to pay and you pay the price not in the palace but on the street. You may not be born with the silver spoon but work your way to dine with those born with the 'golden spoon'. You hustle your way with grit and hard work. You envisage the future you want for yourself and you work it out.

You may have to work the soil, but through study, mentorship, hard work, and unwavering determination, you make a barren land like the garden of the lord.

The world needs these people. They are the engine of any nation's industrial growth. They are not prince but the palace is not complete without them. They may not own a company but run companies. They are found at the top echelon of the corporate world. They are managers of resources and specialists in certain fields of human endeavor. They are the grease that lubricates the economy of any nation. Their domain is their knowledge therefore they seek to expand their knowledge base.

Just like Daniel, they would never forget what takes them to stand before the king in the first instance. They would not say because they have gotten to the apex of their career, it is now time for them to be complacent. They invest much in themselves to remain relevant kings after kings.

Being a noble in a big empire may be preferable to being a village head of one obscure and poor village in that empire.

Being a Man is not a title but a responsibility. A responsibility that Adam bequeaths to us. The Man in the Garden is to work and dress the garden. Age does not make you a Man; work does. What passage of time does is to make an old, tired, grumpy, and sorrowful mere man. It is work that makes you either a king or a noble. Dedication and Diligence make Man.

Mere men lack both Dedication and Diligence. They are doing something quite alright but the thing they are doing is not out of conviction but out of fear, confusion, and compromise. To make matters worse, they are doing it halfheartedly.

That's why they're at the lowest rung of the societal ladder. They're not recognized because they never stood for anything.

They are the first to complain and pass the buck. They want the best but are not willing to give a dime. You see them everywhere occupying space without adding anything.

They're different from a child because a child can still outgrow the stunted growth with right medication and therapy but in their own case, they need to retrace their steps where they miss it and genuinely start anew.

They need to work on themselves and do away with their victim and their entitlement mentality. They need to become a child again and work their butt off or they can just align with Eccl. 9:10.

A child is someone with the potential to be king but lacks the discipline of diligence and thus remains a child Gal. 4: 1.

Age does not make a man; there are many adults in the world today who are babies. Their growth is stunted by fear and people's opinions. They have great dreams and would have gone to achieve majestic things but they are too full of themselves. They weigh themselves down with many impersonal and unnecessary worries like what people would think, what if I fail, what it didn't work out, etc. These unnecessary and impersonal worries obese them to the point of keeping them stuck to their bed of wishful thinking.

Don't allow the thought of death stop you from living.

A grown-up is someone who has reached the age of responsibility, i.e., old enough to make decisions. For some countries, the age starts at 18years, while for the rest, it is 21years. Your voice is respected as an adult. You can vote, you can enter into legally binding contract and you can own property in your name. Most teenagers cannot wait to reach 18, because, they can now determine their lives by themselves. Adulthood is a thing of pride, with endless possibilities. I used to believe so until I started seeing some 50-something-year-old babies, some 37 years old who have surrendered the freedom of decision-making that they naturally attained some 19 years back. All because they are responsibility-shy.

How old are you? I don't mean the number but how much of Purpose you have attained? Do you even know your purpose at all? I am not trying to vilipend you; if there's something I want you to know is that it is not too late.

It doesn't matter how many years you have wasted; the few remaining are more decisive. Jacob was nothing at 80 years old when he discovered his Purpose, he still went ahead to achieve all that GOD said about him. Abraham was 75 years old when GOD called him to his Purpose, yet, he still fathered nations.

No matter how far you think you have gone astray from your purpose, just like the Sun or the Moon, you will always see it when you just look up into your heart.

Your purpose is always inside of you; it is your identity. The gift of the Lord is without repentance Rm. 11: 29. However, your impact, reward, and opportunity dwindle over time that you delay. You may even run out of time.

Nobody is both obliged to be free and also earn a living **Anonymous**

SECTION TWO

I:

Contemporary Problem.

Moses survived the pogrom and infanticide. Daniel survived the massacre of the Babylonians. Joseph could have been killed but for the divine intervention of brother Reuben. David survived Saul's many attempts on his life.

You, also, have survived uncountable attempts on your life. You're the only surviving soul out of hundreds of millions of possible souls. The sperm cell that fertilized your mum's egg was one out of hundreds of million, and that one, is you; the rest died away. It wasn't for strength; it wasn't that you were the smartest but it was GOD being particular that it must be you.

For every 10 children born the same way you're born, 2 children never lived past age 5; of the remaining that survived, about 4-5 million died annually between the age of 5 and 25 years from 1990 and 2014. You are looking at over 100 million of your mates worldwide, that didn't die as an infant but never made it past the age of 25 years.

What makes you this special? You're a lone survivor among 500 million sperm cells, you survived the death that killed 20% of new births and children, and you're not among the over 100 million of your mates that died between ages 5 and 25 years.

That GOD kept you alive today, means only one thing; you're needed. You carry a solution to a living problem; this is the basis for your living Ps 115: 17.

You are living not because of pure luck, not because you're careful not because you deserve it. There are over one thousand and one ways to die but only one way to live. That you are alive today means that you've survived the over a thousand odds that were against you. The odds stacked up against you are too numerous and too powerful for you to survive on your own for a second, GOD kept you alive. You're more than a conqueror.

Your life is the token that you are needed. It shows that you're a potential solution to a living problem. You're alive because of what you carry not what you're. You are a human being, not human meat.

You're a solution to contemporary problems.

GOD told Abraham in Gen. 15: 13, that his children shall be in a strange land for 400 years, guess when the 400 years came? It came at Moses' generation.

GOD said Israel would be captive in Babylon for 70years Jeremiah 29:10. At exactly 70years, Daniel, Nehemiah, Zerubbabel, Ezra, and others decided to take the bull by the horn to make the Will of GOD as prophesized concerning them, come to pass 1Chro 12:32, 2 Sam 5:24.

Is your community or generation grappling with a challenge, lack, or situation that has deferred solution? Are you and your people suffering any nagging problem? The truth is that every contemporary problem has a contemporary solution in that environment and you may be the one carrying the solution.

Israel was wasted for 7years by the Midianites they were

living inside caves like mountain goats.

They prayed, fasted, and even made sacrifices; but what it took for them to be delivered laid with a regular guy who didn't look like it; Gideon, your normal regular guy, a Mr. nobody: without power, without connection, without any clout of importance and worse still, an idol worshipper, yet he delivered the people.

How?

He's done living in caves like others; he was done wishing others would do something; he was done complaining. He knew it wasn't right for the problem to have lasted this long without a solution. He was so convinced that he challenged GOD by recalling the more impossible things GOD did in the past.

You're as culpable as anyone for that challenge your nation, your generation, your community is grappling with right now. You may not be the direct cause but you carry a solution lacking. The solution you carry may address the challenges directly or address the carrier of the solution. The solution to the problem in your environment; is on board not abroad, and you're part of it.

The most amazing thing about the story of Gideon was that the Angel that talked with him didn't give him anything special but just told him to go in his might i.e., how GOD had made him.

How many times the Angels of the Lord is telling you that you don't need anything extra to become what GOD has made you to be? How far have you prolonged the suffering of your people because you just sit there complaining when you can do something about the situation by working out what is inside you?

I don't know how much time you have, but it is not too late for you to rise and be who you are, Lk. 13: 6 - 9.

When you're absent in your place of assignment, simple things become fatally impossible.

I have never seen or heard where GOD raised the dead to solve any nation's problem Lk. 16: 31; the solution you're looking for is on board not abroad. Stop wishing that someone should do something. If it bothers you, it should bring out the best in you.

You're a living solution to a living problem.

That you can see, it means you can do something more than complaining about it. You just need to use the little power you have to set off a chain reaction.

What are those problems that are confronting your environment, for which you wish you had the power to do something?
The truth is that you have the power to do something about it. You just go in this your might; you'll be amazed what GOD would do through you Jud. 7: 1 - 7.

Gideon wasn't JESUS, he wasn't Samuel, he wasn't Samson and definitely, he wasn't John the Baptist. He was a regular guy just like you and I, but he didn't stop at complaining about the problem of his time and didn't allow his limitations and the factors speaking against him like his sinful background, to dictate what he'd do. At the end of the day, out of the population of Israelites existing at that time, it's only his name that stands immortal in our minds today.

Ask yourself, why should a problem be particular to a group of people if the solution is not from among them? Why should something you can't do anything about be there to stop you? Why should you be held accountable for failure you cannot avoid? What kind of a Father would deliberately and needlessly set up his children for failure? Are you calling GOD a sadist?

You could've been born anywhere and at any time on the face of the earth, yet, you're this particularly defined; you think it is inconsequential?

There's a difference between when you are not made for your locality and when your locality is not made for you. Let me explain in detail to you.

When you're not made for a locality means the problem lies with the locality and the people. You look at yourself, you wish you were in a more stable, nicely setup and developed area such that you could give your best. It is common that everyone in that community is complaining about the same thing, if they have the means like you do, they would love to leave that community. The people there believe the solution to the problem is abroad, thus, they spend their time hoping, praying and complaining. You also have imbibed the culture of learned helplessness; you have conditioned your mind to relocate yourself from that environment because you believe that GOD made a blunder making you the citizen of that community. You have an ego problem.

When that locality is not made for you is when you're the

problem because what you need to be what GOD has made you for, when what your heart beats for, is not in that environment or when your dream and creativity would be stifled by that environment.

Among these two scenarios, under which condition are you justified to relocate? The answer is found in Matt. 5: 13 – 14. If you're in an environment that would stifle your imagination, i.e., a locality that is not made for you, the best thing to do is to leave there before you lose your saltness. If, however, the environment is the fault, if you feel you're too good for that area; then, maybe, GOD didn't make a mistake after all, maybe, GOD creates you as a light for that environment. All you need to do is just to do what is natural to you, just shine. And when you do, GOD would find a way to make your light never grow dim.

Exercise:

List 5 present challenges facing your country, community, world.
List 5 of your strengths.
Under each challenge, write how your strength can become useful.

2:

Family, Ethnic or Geography Specialization

Moses, Aaron, Children of Issachar and Samuel

That Moses and Aaron were of the tribe that GOD would choose as priest wasn't by accident; GOD doesn't do anything adlibbed. GOD had already set it out before the foundation that the tribe of Levi would burn incense before HIM. GOD had it all planned out that Moses, Aaron, Samuel (1 Chr. 6: 16 – 28), John the Baptist all come from no other tribe than that of Levi.

There are certain profession, vocation and purpose that predominantly runs through your family, ethnicity, race, location, etc. It is therefore a wise thing to consider if your calling is from the dominant calling of the particular groupings you belong to. Take, for example, Track and field is usually dominated by blacks while long-distance running has Kenyan and Ethiopians as dominants. Argentina and Brazil would always produce great footballers, while Germans and Japanese makes great machines. Indians, Israelis, Koreans, Americans, and Singaporeans are known for ICT. Chinese, and Japanese, are known for technology. A small

Fulani boy can herd cattle from Senegal through Nigeria to Cameroon, a journey of about 5000km. You will also observe that some tribes are good in business while some are good in administration and some Military.

As nations have a comparative advantage over others in certain things, so also some family have advantages in some trade or vocations. Some people will say it topography, socialization, habitat and other factors that give you the advantage; but who made the topography? Who decides which environment to be born into? If things beyond your control make us fit for a particular thing, then, can we all agree that there's something you're fashioned for?

Look at your family: nuclear and extended, what are those vocation that runs through the family? Your mum was good at that, your uncle the same, and now, you are being drifted to that line. Do you know that a certain vocation will not leave your family until it is fulfilled?

Someone has already blazed a trail for you; who knows what you might find when you walk the track. You might find your path or a part of your path.

David wanted to build a tabernacle for GOD but it's his son, Solomon, who ended up building it.

GOD told Abraham that his children would be slaves in Egypt for 400 years, thereafter, HE would come to rescue them and bring them to the land HE promised him. It means GOD already engaged the proposed family for the next 500 years at least; meaning that there's a transgenerational purpose for the family

HE's about to establish.

Had Moses been privy to this information; had he sat with the elders to discuss how they became slaves in Egypt; he'd have seen that his urge, his nagging desire to see the people saved from their misery of slavery is a long time coming. He'd have understood that he was not nursing a Personal Assignment but a Lineage one.

This would have helped in no small way in crystalizing his mandate earlier and avoided the extra and needless 70 wasted years. GOD wanted them to be in the promised land at the 400th year, but they did so in 470th year. This was not the perfect will of GOD for them. Many people destined to make it to the promised land died in the desert including Moses.

When you compare this with what happened in the time of Daniel, Nehemiah about 800 years later, you'd appreciate the importance of knowing if there's any subsisting Generational or Lineage assignment and how that knowledge can alter the destiny of any nation, Daniel 9: 2.

Sometimes, it is not only prayer, sacrifice, and worship you need. You also need to know if there's a hanging assignment on your family, your nation, and your generation; so that your 400 years won't turn to 470 years or never.

You can know if there's a hanging assignment over your life, by having a conversation with your parents. Ask them what else would they be doing if they had not chosen the career path they took. Ask them if there's something they regret not following through on or if there was a call, or a purpose they regretted not going after.

You may find out that they had the same panting, the same calling or desire you're having right now. You may be surprised how similar your 'dreams' are to that of your parents'. This is called Lineage Assignment. It's different from Individual Assignments. And, until someone in that lineage fulfills that assignment, nobody would be able to achieve their assignments easily because every individual assignment in that family is a branch from a tree of that Lineage Assignment.

The children of Issachar were reputed to know what to do per time i.e., they had a discerning spirit. The question to ask is what about Issachar himself?

Issachar was likened to an ass, a beast of burden that couldn't take any initiative but rather depended on physical strength than mental or spiritual strength. Issachar never became what GOD wanted for him but his children succeeded where he failed.

Don't underestimate the place of Family, Ethnic Specialization in what you're made to be. Although it is not every Levite that went on to be Prophet, some remained sons of the Prophets, some did not even officiate at the altar. The most important thing is to ask yourself if your heart beats for what runs in your lineage, ethnicity or in your nation.

You can also know your Purpose when you explore what is in abundance in your environment. This thing in abundance should not be something that is in vogue. This is because GOD is not moved by popular opinion but by faith.

Faith makes you trust GOD so much as to believe HE had settled you 2 Pet. 1: 3. There's good in every land, it takes a willing mind to see it Is 1:19.

The same way everyone can discover his purpose from the nagging challenge of a community is also the same way anybody can derive his purpose from the abundant resources in that community.

This is why you'd see high unemployment rate in areas with abundant natural resources that is not being processed but exported out as a commodity.

GOD has schemed out everything including you and has masterfully aligned everything towards an end; If only you would explore the resources in your environment; (the less popular with the people, the better it is) you would have gone more than a mile in discovering your Purpose here on earth.

The fact that you're able to see what is right under your feet; shows that you have it in your heart.

Exercise:

List 10 uniqueness skills or attributes of your country or tribe, which of these do you have and how can you develop a vocation from it like your countrymen?

Look at your environment, what do you have in abundant that other environments lack and you have the mix of temperament to explore?

List out the common vocations in your family, do you have a suppressed passion for any? If you don't, can you build vocation around any? Or can you build a whole new vocation from the skills needed to perform that vocation?

The greatest tragedy of the family is the unlived lives of the parents.

Carl Gustav Jung

You are not the product of your environment; you are the product for your

environment.

3:

Through Dreams

Jacob, Joseph and Peter Experience

A lot of academic theories on dreams are purely under the realm of psychological predispositions. Sigmund's theory that, dreams are repressed wishes only captures an aspect of the 3 aspects of dream.

There are 3 aspects or sources of dreams: your physical being (Self), your emotion (Satan), and your Subconscious (Divine). You don't joke with any dream you cannot link to your physical condition. Dreams from the emotion and the subconscious are just tips of the iceberg; they carry much more than the eyes can see. They act like computer code which tell the computer what to do. But computer codes can be virus, trojan or an application program. Let's look at them and see what you are expected to do in each case.

3 Sources of Dream

<u>Physical</u>

Physical being as a source or trigger for your dream occurs because of your repressed wishes. It is when biological needs are not vented, making it to linger on in your brain. So, when you sleep, your brain, in an attempt of declogging itself, clear the cache currently stored on the memory, the resultant effect is the images you see when you sleep. This usually happens during the REM (Rapid Eye Movement), i.e., when you are about to wake up; it constitutes about 5% of dream for most adult.

Examples of such dream are: wet dreams (when your sexual desire or needs are not being vented), eating in dreams (when you slept hungry), dreams about water (when you need to urinate), and dreaming about what you wished for before sleeping. Any dream that you can easily trace back to your physical, biological and mental state Eccl. 5: 3, has nothing to worry about. Sigmund Freud's and other psychological analysis work are of this nature.

<u>Evil</u>

Most dream that involves fear, lust, pride, hatred, vengeance, hopelessness, helplessness or when you give up something precious or when you miss your way, you were bitten by dog, snake, or dog barking at you, you were naked, you were stopped from moving forward not from danger, you were afraid upon seeing uniform men, you're pressed in your sleep by incubus or succubus or any other nightmarish dream; any non-REM dream (dream in a state of deep sleep, dream in which it is the occurrence in the dream like fear, gasping for breath, sorrow, running for dear life etc. that jolts you back to life).

Through evil dreams, some people have been remote-controlled into death, some into crime unwittingly, some into lost of opportunity, while some were first swindled of their hard-earned money in their dream, before making bad investment is real life.

Nothing just happens. Everything that happens had existed in the spiritual realm before being transmuted into the physical. As you should know this already, energy can neither be created nor be destroyed but can only be transformed. Every event in your life is the energy that existed in the spiritual which you transmuted into reality through the portal of dreams and work.

Your Power over Evil Dream:

Power of whatever happens in your life is yours except you relinquish that power. That you have evil dream does not mean you would certainly experience evil. Evil dream, just like quarks, needs certain conditions to become matter, if starved of those conditions, it would only exist as possibility or a dark cloud which would eventually pass away.

There are certain things you can do and 3 prime things are hinted below:

> You should exercise your authority by condemning it. It is said in Is. 54:17 that thou condemn every negative pronouncement against you by yourself. You don't need anyone to do that on your behalf; even if anyone does so for you, it cannot be as definitive as the one done by you.

> Secondly, you must run from evil so as not to give the dream the right or authority Is. 49: 24. You cannot condemn evil dream, condemn lost, death and every negative pronouncement of dream and yet frolic with sin. You are making yourself a willing captive.

Then, get busy working out the good seeds in you so as not to give chance to the devil to perform its enterprise. Matt. 16: 19 and Amos 3: 3. The blessing in Isaiah 49: 1 – 13 is only for those are living according to the purpose of GOD.

<u>Divine</u>

Jacob had a dream that showed him his Purpose in Gen. 28: 18. GOD showed him a ladder that reaches unto heaven and angels ascending and descending. The dream shows that he'd start off a process that would reconcile man to GOD.

I always tell people that GOD still speaks through dreams, Satan does and also does your body. That Satan quotes the Bible does not give him ownership. It is your responsibility to know which is which. Thankfully, it is not impossible to do.

2 Reasons God Speaks Through Dream

The first thing to know is that GOD usually speaks in dreams to people who are yet to mature spiritually and to people who don't give GOD enough attention in their daily activities but they are crucial in what GOD is about to do.

GOD spoke to Jacob a lot of the time through dreams. GOD spoke to Pharaoh, to Abimelech, to Nebuchadnezzar, to Joseph, to the Magi, to Joseph the husband of the virgin Mary, to Laban and so on. You will notice that most, if not all, that GOD spoke to through dreams were spiritually not yet matured. That doesn't mean that

GOD doesn't speak to HIS elect through dreams, it is just that they depend more on other ways. Nm 12: 6-7.

Another reason is that, GOD would speak to you through dreams if you have to pass through fire on the way to the fulfillment of your destiny. Or if what GOD wants to tell you is too complex or too bulky, so, GOD burns it into the disc of your heart through dreams. This is important because as the event unfolds, even though you have the feeling of déjà vu, you won't fret because you already know what to do or the outcome.

This, also, confirms that, you perfectly align with GOD's purpose for your life. An example that comes to mind is Joseph. If not for the dream, Joseph would have lost his purpose of being the earthly father of JESUS Christ. He'd have break up with Mary but for the dream he had.

Look at Pharaoh. It wasn't that Pharaoh was righteous but he occupies a pole position in the plan of GOD for the earth and most especially for Abraham. GOD spoke to Pharaoh for HIS Elect sake.

8 Ways to know it is GOD speaking to you

The articles in your dream. What do you see in your dream? What are those things that form the background of the dream? What is the condition like, the setting, the ambience and the other things in the dream apart from the dream?

Is the atmosphere enervating or depressing? Is it peaceful or chaotic? is the background welcoming or beggarly?

David said in Psalms: thou make me to lie down in green pasture and thou restore my soul: if the you don't feel restored, refreshed and enervated in your dream, then it's probably not from GOD. Another thing to use to decipher what the source of your dream is, is the voice of a renowned prophet confirming what is in the Bible, or you see Dove, Heaven (the throne of GOD), you hear songs of Praise and Worship, you feel Peace, a Bible passage into your heart, or you see Sunshine that is refreshing, gentle flowing crystal-clear river, a Lamb, a big welcoming tree, the hand of GOD, purifying fire or fire that is not destructive.

When you see any of these, in your dream, the things that represent GOD, HIS holiness, or giving glory to GOD or you have the feeling of Peace. When you encounter any of these things in your dream, then, it is safe to accept the dream as being from GOD.

The 2nd condition is that that dream has nothing to do with your feelings, what you want and definitely, not in things you can control physically. You can also know when GOD is speaking to you through dream if what you dream about is against your natural desire or wish. If your dream does not align with what you know, belief or conditioned to accept as the norm. an example is Peter and the unclean vessel in Acts 10. It would not contradict the Bible but may contradict tradition and custom.

The 3rd is that the dream from GOD will have a meaning and be definitive: Every dream from GOD would have meaning which you would be able to decode. You may not be able to decode the meaning immediately but if you can sit down, the meaning and expectation would begin to crystalize. And if it is too complex for you to decode because you don't have HIS Spirit in you, then someone with HIS Spirit close to you should be able to.

Furthermore, you would know if the dream is from GOD when the atmosphere in the dream is peaceful, calming, invigorating, assuring and also when the dream feels real, not threatening and you are not under any kind of human limitation.

You will also know if the dream is from GOD when your waking life is about peace, Joy and thanksgiving. You feel the sense of the supernatural around you.

GOD will confirm it. Acts 10: 30-32

It is trance-like. When you are not sleeping nor awake but you have this out-of-the-body experience, then GOD is telling you something. Or when you hardly lie down to sleep and you start dreaming, Jacob's encounter with the heavenly follows this pattern. Hardly had he slept that he dreamt.

And lastly, the dream is a warning, especially concerning things you desire. GOD can warn you against your intended, GOD can warn against certain actions. GOD can warn you against evil coming your way. The truth is that if GOD would warn you, GOD would make it so clear that if you can think on it, both the subject (area of your life) and the action (what to do) would be clear.

3 Types of godly dream

Godly dreams can broadly be categorize into 3, depending on if GOD: wants to inform you, inspire you, or to warn you.

Knowing what GOD wants to achieve (the types the dream is), is sine qua non to knowing the necessary steps expected of you. There're some dreams that comes with an obligation of what to do to make it be fulfilled; some, obligation on what to do to stop it from happening, while some, you may not be able to stop it nor facilitate it.

Let's consider what these dreams are and how you can ride upon them to your glory.

1. Informative Dream:

There are times when GOD has made up HIS mind about accomplishing certain things through you; GOD showing the dream to you through dream is not to seek your permission but these following reasons.

a. To act as a signpost on your way to your divine purpose so that when you see the dreams being fulfilled, you'd know where you are in GOD's scheme of things. This dream usually precedes trials, temptation, test and misfortunes. Joseph just dreamt that he would be great in life but what happens next was non sequitur. Immediately Joseph had that dream, all hell broke. For no reason whatsoever, he started walking into dangers; everything points him out as the evil man who the gods are fighting against.

Whenever you have a dream of a great future for yourself, not that you concoct it in your head, and there's no obligation; know that you are about being led into the wilderness to be tempted as JESUS was.

b. After withstanding that initial loss of things, the next test would be from the member of your household, those people that you hold in high esteem, those you depend on or draw strength from, would stand like Mrs. Job to question the importance of your existence. They are your friends like Eliphaz, Bildad and Zophar, they love you so much as Peter love JESUS so much that he didn't want Christ to die yet, he denied HIM later on. To overcome this stage to your breakthrough, you need an incurable holy stubbornness inside you. The truth is that you cannot withstand the trial that is on your way; the only people that would remain with you, after the challenge has sieved away your fair whether friends, the people that has now become the only source of your strength, those you totally depend on, would come at you, they would tell you to deny GOD and die, they would tell you to your face that you are suffering because of your evil deed and so on; just to dissuade you from the glory.

I must confess to you, I can't tell you what you'd face, that is why the dream is given to you. the dream is not ordinary, it is not only to show you your glorious future but also implanting a 'new spirit' like that of Elisha, Joshua, David, Joshua, Job and Joseph, a never say die attitude.

c. And lastly, it would be unwonted of GOD to show you that kind of dream, infuse you with the resoluteness without capability to achieve it. GOD didn't give David the dream that he would become the king of Israel one day only to drive him to be killed by Goliath. GOD didn't show Joseph that glorious future without planting someone like the cupbearer, who would speak for him before Pharaoh when the right time comes, in his life.

Everything you'd need to actualize the dream, from right connection to the right attitude, from charisma to wealth, from temperament to right location and as many as over one million factors that must perfectly aligned, are all sorted during the dream.

2. Warning/Instructive Dream

GOD would use dream to warn you about certain action you're about to take especially those action that are destiny shaping or whose consequence can be severe.

You may want to take up a job or sign a contract, and while you are about to, you just remembered a dream you had sometimes ago where you missed your way; or you are thinking of getting married and in that period, you dreamt you fell into a ditch or you saw yourself sitting at the back of your fiancé car, sandwiched among his brothers and sisters while his mum was sitting comfortable at the front seat. If you go ahead and marry such a person, don't be surprised if he does not give you adequate attention or you lack joy and fulfilment in your marriage.

Career choice, Marriage partner choice, and Location, are the 3 fundamental choices. They represent the Garden, Eve and Eden. When you want to take steps towards any of the these 3 and there's no clearcut direction from GOD as regarding them, then go into the archive of your heart and see if GOD had not spoken about it in your dream.

You can never pray against a dream that came as a warning from GOD. It is not every dream you can cast and bound. If it is from GOD, the best you can do is to ask GOD for what to do.

Please, take note of the caveat here. Some dreams though would show you negative thing about what you intend to do, yet, it doesn't mean you should not go ahead. Sometimes, the dream might come as the result of fear of the unknown, sometimes, Satan would even come up those dreams just to make you lose out on GOD's purpose for your life. If you have read 'How to know it is GOD speaking to you' in the preceding section, then you should not have any problem discerning which.

3. Inspiration/Teaching

Dream that teaches you what you never came across, that shows you alternative or creative way of solving a nagging problem or that reveals to you evil plan against you and how to defuse it or just stir up your creative imagination, artistic flair, scientific and technological inventiveness, or tell. Inspirational dream shows you what to do by showing you the alternative, creative or out of the box way of achieving

So many people have discovered answers to agelong mysteries in their dreams. Some have found solutions to real problems in their dreams, some have thought out inventions and scientific breakthroughs while asleep. Albert Einstein generate idea on speed of light through dream, Dmitri Mendeleev saw how to arrange the periodic table in dream, Samuel Taylor got inspiration for Kubla Khan through dream, Paul McCartney of the Beetles got inspiration for his classic: Let It Be, through dream, the sewing machine needle was a product of dream, Niels Bohr groundbreaking theory on atomic structure was gained while dreaming, Srinivasa Ramanujan's number theory, analysis and many of his contributions in mathematics were given to him in dreams.

Why bad dreams fulfil more than good dreams

Bad dreams get fulfilled more than the good ones in the ratio 8:2. For most people, they don't take glorious dream seriously because they know from experience that even their almost certain success or breakthrough in real life becomes complicated and futile immediately they dream they finally succeed. But let this people have a small bad dream, they start running helter-skelter. The reason, their bad or evil dream is like a determined reality to them.

Bad dreams are like tares that the enemy came and spread unto the field and went his way. The enemy didn't have to do more than this; no need to till, weed, fertilize, yet, the weed would grow. Even without rain for several years, weeds would sprout up and grow at the sight of the first rain. That is why you don't ignore bad dreams; it can be transgenerational. Not doing anything, it will grow, doing something, it will still grow. The right action is to work on the seed. Yes, you can reject every evil dream, affirm your desire; nothing is guarantee if you don't do like Jacob in Gen. 28: 18. Jacob had a dream about his future; despise his present predicament, Jacob set up an altar with the promise to build a temple there when he returned. Jacob did not dwell on what GOD said about him, Jacob cooperated with GOD for the fulfilment. What you do immediately GOD show you HIS intention, would go a long way to determine if you'd attain it easily or not.

Stop sharing your dream with anyone instead step into it.

GOD shows you that you'd be great one day, start today by building yourself. GOD shows you, you will travel over the world, start by learning new languages. Start the process, work the work, don't think the thought. Don't dream and walk away thinking you have that in the bag already. Remember, it is only weed that grow by itself not seed. What GOD says is seed; what Satan plan is weed, Matt. 13: 25.

<u>Exercise:</u>

What dream has been so consistent with you that provoke deep emotional reaction like crying or rejoicing from the dream state to life?

What dream do you feel satisfied with or your peace is not disturbed?

What do you see yourself doing in your dream state that you feel really good about yourself?

Until you make the unconscious conscious, it will direct your life and you will

call it FATE.

Carl Jung

He said, "Listen to my words: "when there is a prophet among you, I, the

LORD, reveal myself to them in vision, I speak to them in dreams.

Numbers 12: 6

For God does speak – now one way, now another – though no one

perceives it. In a dream, in a vision of the night...

Job 33: 14 – 15a

The ancient knew something, which we seem to have forgotten

Albert Einstein

Dream is like an antenna that tentacled into forgotten knowledge

that is sealed up until such a time like this.

4

Where you are favoured.

Human beings, naturally, are self-centered and selfish. It takes more than meeting the eye for someone you don't know from anywhere to delight to help you. It is uncommon for someone to inconvenience him or herself to bring you up to your high place.

Favour is a sign of GOD's approval.

Favour performs 3 functions:

Number one is that **Favour empowers.** GOD favours men to give them what they need to fulfil their assignment here on earth.

In the time of Nehemiah, the king issued an order and sealed the order with his signet (the sign of his authority) and gave it to Nehemiah; with that, Nehemiah had everything he needed to fulfil his mandate. When Pharaoh elevated Joseph, Pharaoh changed his raiment and gave him a scepter to rule.

The scepter of your authority is the honour which GOD favours you with. You cannot be following GOD's will and goodness and mercy would not follow you. This is an aberration. Favour is GOD's signet that HE gives to whomever is on the go with his/her purpose on earth.

Lack of Favour cast aspersion on your Mandate.

Favour is not an 'Art' but GOD's Pact with human to fulfil the Part of HIS

Favour is not deserved; it is served. It is not worked for; it is worked with. It is not attained; it is obtained. It is given by the SOMEONE who has the power to control the mind of whom that cannot be bought to serve someone who has sold his life to HIM.

Show me a self-made man; and you have shown me one who has made himself nothing.

If everything you have; you have to struggle or pay through your nose to get it; it may be that you're not walking in the Purpose of GOD Ps. 127: 2.

Another thing favour does is to **show GOD's gratitude** towards whom is working out the seeds of GOD in them. When you do what GOD creates you for, you delight HIM and HE in return delights to honour you Es. 6: 6a.

And lastly, **favour affirms**.

The Egyptians just lost their firstborn, they had every reason to hate the Israelites with passion but because the Israelis were in GOD's Purpose for them, the Egyptians had no option but to 'willingly' give out the best of the clothes, jewelry, spices, etc. to them.

If that is not Favour, tell me what it is.

Favour is GOD affirming that HE's happy with you.

It wasn't ordinary that grown men would abandon their lives in the city and came to the wilderness with their entire family, to pledge their loyalty to a fugitive in the person of David who was barely 20years old at that time 1Sam 22: 2.

GOD is sending you burden sharer, which is a pointer that GOD doesn't want you to fail.

The prime help or burden sharer GOD would send to you is your Eve. GOD said that it wasn't good for Adam to be the only one to face the assignment all by himself. GOD reasoned that HE would give him someone that would lighten his burden, so that, whenever Adam sees her, he sees GOD's approval.

GOD didn't create gender for definition but for identification. What GOD created for definition was Adam (the worker of the garden) and Eve (the helper) to achieve that Purpose. Eve's role in this world is to be a helpmeet, a burden-sharer, a sign of GOD's approval and of perfection, not a competitor Pr. 18: 22.

That being said, one way you'd know that the thing you hold as your Purpose is true or not, is if your spouse has a buy-in or buy into it.

Let's assume that your spouse doesn't agree with you on your Purpose (no buy-in) but s/he doesn't stand in your way but instead makes it easier for you to pursue it, just as Peter's wife and Joseph, the husband of, Mary the mother of JESUS did, then you have got a spouse that buys into it. When you're following after your Purpose; Favour would naturally follow you Ps. 23,

If your spouse neither have a buy-in nor buy into it, it is either you have missed your Eve or you have missed your purpose.

Let me add a caveat here. Like every good thing, there's usually a fake of it. Some favour can be bought as Abraham bought favour with Pharaoh in Gen. 12: 16.

GOD made it abundantly clear to Abraham that he was 'useless' to HIM without Sarah Gen. 17: 15–22. Imagine exchanging something as dear as that for sheep and goat; you call that favour? That's a misnomer.

You must know the source of the favour before you can use it to know if you're working out your Purpose or not.

You cannot call it a sign from GOD when you merit it or as a result of expectation for future gain. You cannot be a sinner and expect GOD to favour you. This is a steep end Ps. 37.

Also, people rejecting you might have nothing to do with ill-favour but it is a phase of your NIGHT time. Interpret the favour you receive responsibly. It is not an end in itself but a means.

Exercise:

What is that advantage you have that is not common?

Where is that advantage useful?

Among the 'hobbies' you have, which of them does the unique favour you enjoy gratify?

Favour is not a commodity to consume but a resource to deploy.

You can gauge GOD's satisfaction by the unmerited favour you enjoy but that's not all about it.

5

The advantage your position conveys.

Moses, Nehemiah and Esther's Experiences

Moses being adopted and trained in Egypt by Pharaoh's daughter means that he was a Prince. The same incident played out in the lives of Esther and Nehemiah.

God have a culture of putting his people in power or around the corridor of power so that at the auspicious moment, they use the advantage, privilege and paraphernalia of office for HIS purpose.

GOD put Nehemiah in the position of king's butler to checkmate Sanballat and Tobias. GOD made Mordecai a gateman at Shushan to grant him privileged access to the palace that Esther would later explore to become queen and thereafter save the people from Haman's genocide. GOD made Moses to be a prince in Egypt to give him privileged access to Pharaoh. Without Moses, who would have gotten access to Pharaoh, let alone asked him to release the people? Moses, being Pharaoh's brother, had access to him which no one else had.

GOD does not need you because you're in power; GOD puts you in power because HE needs you.

There are some things you have that others don't. You're a queen to King Ahasuerus in Vashti's stead for a purpose; you might not comprehend it now. You have been empowered for certain obligations GOD has set you for. It is not by your power you get to that position; it is not any godfather; GOD orchestrated things to bring you to that position for certain tasks that are coming your way. It is for HIS pleasure, Rev. 4: 11.

You're not the best; but the perfect fit.

You can see that the whole essence of Mordecai getting the job at the palace was to save Israel later on. It wasn't because he was the most qualified but because it had to be him because of Esther. Esther wasn't the most beautiful girl at that time but she possessed the right mix of temperament, upbringing, gift, faith etc., to nullify Haman's threat. Esther was just perfect to be the queen at that time so also was Mordecai as gateman.

Any advantage, any office, any privilege, any skill, any position, any location that GOD gives to you; will either metamorphose into your purpose or lead you to it. As long as it is GOD that gives it to you, your calling is within it or just around the corner Mk 12: 1 - 9.

Every assignment precedes the assignee. And everything happening in the life of the assignee prepares him/her for the assignment.

BE PRUDENT

There is a need to be discreet in using your gift or your advantage. I have seen many people who either lost the advantage of their life trying to be a hero because they are not circumspective.

There is a difference between a need and a purpose. Understanding this difference would decide if you'd achieve your purpose or not.

Your gift is not for show-off. It is not to be used at every risen need. You can't be capricious or daring with your gift. GOD instructed Joseph to run to Egypt with JESUS because of a mere mortal.

Despite her power and influence, Esther did not bother to use it to elevate Mordecai's (her foster father) rank and position in the palace.

Don't lose the advantage before you need it. Samson was so irresponsible and vindictive with his gift that he died without accomplishing his purpose nor anyone take over from him.

Unless someone runs to you for help like that Canaanite woman in Matt. 15: 22 - 27, you don't just give your gift without being prompted by the giver.

When Mary begged her Son for a miracle at a marriage in Cana, JESUS didn't oblige her until GOD gave HIM a go-ahead, Jn 2.

<u>Exercise:</u>

What is abundant in and around you?

What can you make with it?

Which of the things you can make, does your heart really beats for?

I must be willing to give up what I am in order to become what I will be.

Albert Einstein

The privilege of a lifetime is to become who you truly are

Carl Jung

Better is the enemy of good

Voltaire

6

The advantages your limitation confers.

Moses' Experience

Moses, your normal regular guy: his biggest challenge then was being accepted by his people. Moses was born a Jew; raised an Egyptian didn't even know anything about the GOD of his fathers; how was he supposed to lead the people he knew nothing about? To make matters worse, Moses had a speech problem.

When Moses heeded the calling, these supposed limitations became a factor that opened the door and gave him an unrestrained audience with Pharaoh.

The first disadvantage that GOD used was his upbringing. Understand that while Moses was in the Palace, he was being prepped to be the head of the Egyptian army the same way Ramsey was being prepped to be Pharaoh. Even after 40 years, he still commands some clout in Egypt.

Imagine how Ramsey would have acted when the guard told him that Moses was waiting in the courtyard to see him. Which Moses? he would have asked. Moses my brother? Is Moses still alive? Where is he? Why are you keeping him waiting?

If it's not Moses, who would have gone?

Imagine Aaron or any other person walking up to Pharaoh; Pharaoh let my people go? It would be a miracle if the person wasn't beheaded. GOD had it planned out. Moses' birth and upbringing looked like a baggage, a snare, an incubus, but see how GOD used it to achieve HIS purpose.

GOD made and prepared Moses for this role, for 30 years when Moses was purpose-shy like Jonah, no one could take over his role.

Another disadvantage that turned out to prove Moses was the one, was his speech challenge. It was an abomination to stand before Pharaoh and not to be of excellent speech. GOD planned that Moses would stand before Pharaoh one day to demand that the Israelites be let go, yet GOD made him a stutterer.

Do you know that this speech impairment helped Moses in fulfilling his assignment? This disability made it impossible for him to be diplomatic in his speech. This not only confers some credibility but also was daring and authoritative in some way. This made Ramsey, the Pharaoh wonder: (*was had happened to my timid brother Moses? Moses knew the tradition so well that nobody dared look at me in the eyes let alone issue a command. Something is behind this my brother's boldness; I better be diplomatic with Moses and also be strong before my people so that I would not be demystified*). Moses was direct and straightforward with his demand without embellishing anything: *thus say the LORD, let my people go or I will kill your firstborn:* who could have said that to mighty Pharaoh but an impudent, and crude Moses?

The last of the disadvantages that GOD used to achieve His purpose is Moses being a fugitive.

Being a fugitive allowed Moses to reconnect back to GOD's

purpose for his life. During Moses' desert years, he was able to have a soul-searching and truthful conversation with himself about what purpose was to his life. He took stock of his life and wondered how his life was thinning out without anything to show for him being on this earth.

This period in Moses' life was the most testing, yet the learning period of his life. Moses learnt the life-saving skill of surviving in the cruelest environment; Moses learnt patience, Moses learnt humility, Moses learnt hard work, Moses learnt many things he was not exposed to, while growing up in Egypt. Moses came to know GOD personally. Moses, a 'foreigner' became the person who showed GOD's precepts and statutes to the Israelites, all happened in the desert, his NIGHT time.

Initially, it looked as if Moses was disadvantaged. He was seen as an outsider by the Israelis, the Egyptians had passed a death sentence on him, an 80something year old stammerer, yet all these disadvantages were the exact match for the role.

I have said it severally and I am not afraid to say it again here. You don't have any disadvantages. That, which you think is a limitation may be planted by GOD to make you perfect for the purpose HE assigned you for.

No one is truly disabled; everyone is variedly abled for the role GOD has prepared us for.

Look at Shaquille O'Neal and Yao Ming for example, their height could have been a great disadvantage to them. With their height, it was easy to spot them out. They cannot just blend in like most of us could. They just have to take a stand; they don't have any choice.

One thing that this disadvantage afford them is that it straight-jacket them into a vocation. The vocation chose them when most other vocation reject them. The vocation founds them out and because of very little possibility, they settled quite early.

I don't know you but I can guess that you are taller than Lionel Messi. What makes me think so? Well, Lionel Messi is shorter than 70% of most people. While he was small, he suffered a rare disease that caused his abnormal growth. Instead of him lamenting and cursing this misfortune, he built his life upon the foundation that was meant to limit him and this same misfortune made him to be arguably the GOAT in world's football.

Most people who went on to achieve greatness were once people who were limited by skin colour, height, health, resources, status, education, and so on. Their secret lies in their choosing the profession, vocation, career, or business that they're best suited for, not just the one that suits them.

You don't just choose the first thing on the bucket list of the advantages your limitation confers, if so, Lionel Messi would have ended up being a weightlifter, a sprinter, a break dancer, a carpenter, an IT specialist, an accountant and there's no end of what the other him could be. Thank GOD he didn't choose what he could do. He chose football because that's what he's made for, the thing that he's best suited for.

Had he settled to be a weightlifter, he'd be using just his height advantage. Had he chosen to be a breakdancer, he'd be using his nimbleness, had he settled for sprinter, he'd be using his speed. Had he chosen to be an IT specialist or accountant, it is only his analytical mind he'd be using. Football engaged his height, his nimbleness, his speed, his analytical mind, his clear vision, his demeanor, etc. All of these make him to be unique and special.

Imagine Cristiano Ronaldo as a sprinter a swimmer or a model. He could do all these quite well but he'd be underutilizing himself. Or imagine Shaquille O'Neal as a bouncer, a runner or military personnel. Imagine Bill Gates ended up being a lecturer. Imagine the shy Elon Musk ended up a soldier or a pastor?

I am not saying these vocations are bad, they are fantastic, but they are not good enough for the subject we are talking about here. Even when they could have ended up being such because of physical, mental, economic and social limitations, they didn't.

Look at yourself. You have limitations one way or the other. There's no one without one. They're there to tailor and structure you perfectly for just one thing. That one thing your limitation makes you perfect for, is what you're made for; your purpose and your reason for living.

Don't be too quick to pass it off as a statement of what you can or cannot do. You're not disabled; you're made to specification for the special assignment GOD need you for.

When you embrace your so-called limitations; it will become your elevator.

The so-called 'disadvantage' is not meant to limit you in absolute terms but in relative terms. There's a certain thing you're perfect for. It's not meant to stymie you but to focus you. so, do away with that victim mentality. It's time to see you in a new light Jn 9: 1–3.

Out of the many things your limitations have limited you to, take one of them. The one that you're taking may not be the easiest, may not be the one that jumps right at you immediately after you open the box, nor the one that can scream the loudest: me, me, me. Rather, let it be the one that incorporates and maximizes every single thing in you, including your strengths and your weaknesses. This is how Moses got to know what is calling was before his interaction with the bushing bush. This is why we got to know anyone called Lionel Messi, Shaquille O'Neal, and Yao Ming. You could be the next to funnel your Limitations to Strength.

I know your fear is what if my disability doesn't carry any significance?

One of the films I enjoyed watching while growing up was *Back to the Future*. It is about Time Travel in which one can travel through the past or the future to make things work perfectly for that person. It means if there's something you need for a task but you don't have that thing, you can go back in time to get that thing and come to the present with it.

Can you imagine the limited mind of man conceiving such a possibility, Wonderful!

If man's heart can conceive it but GOD cannot do it, then how is HE GOD? How would the omnipotent, omniscient, All in All, timeless, ageless, the Alpha and the Omega; not be able to time-travel your life to make that disability perfect for the future HE thinks towards you?

I don't know what we think about this GOD. We tend to accept HIM with our limited minds. It doesn't matter what disability you have; HE wills it for a purpose Jer. 29: 11.

This is the least of GOD. If you don't believe that you don't have a limitation but a specification, you should stop deceiving yourself and let the whole world know that you're an atheist.

You cannot say you believe that GOD creates you but only a certain part of you; some other parts are created in accidence or by Satan, so it is inauspicious in GOD's agenda. No. it doesn't work that way. You cannot claim the omniscience of GOD and still hold on to the thought that HE is limited.

<u>Exercise:</u>

What is about you that is too difficult for GOD to deal with?

What is that condition of yours that is standing as a limitation or disability?

Can you look through it to see

If we agree that it is GOD that creates everyone in whatever form we're; it will be unjust for GOD to make certain people disadvantaged without making adequate compensation for their inadequacies.

This is not the GOD I have grown to know.

7

Your Temperament

Jacob and Esau's Experience

Jacob was a quiet man meaning he was more phlegmatic than melancholy as his life would reveal. Esau his brother was more social and the outgoing type whose anger burns like fire on a straw – Esau was a sanguine. These 2 brothers' temperaments feature in the factor that determines their lots in life.

Esau as a sanguine was so concerned about today that he sold his birthright for a pot of porridge. Jacob a phlegm was passive about life that at age 80, he didn't have any meaning to life.
GOD made them that way to fit into HIS plan. Their temperament is GOD setting them up for their assignment here on earth.

Temperament is not learnt; it is not inherited and obviously not genetic. Don't mind the so-called scientists that say between 20-60% of temperament is genetic. 20 – 60% is quite large enough to accommodate any event especially when you consider that temperament can be categorize into 2 or 4 broad categories.

I have seen many twins which share similar genetical makeup but of different personality. You'd start seeing a marked difference in them from their early teenage years. One may be outgoing, the other may be reserved, they're not of the same IQ nor interest, so also their approach to life is different. It is quite possible that at an early age, twins might show similar temperament. The reason this happen is that they try to model each other. Later on in life, you will that they're individual and unique as Jacob and Esau. You cannot change your temperament; you can only moderate it. Your temperament is not learnt but the part that GOD made that you came into this world as.

Your calling revolves around your temperament. Your temperament is not a burden, it is not a disadvantage unless when you are trying to be somebody else.

Melancholy

As a melancholy, you are meant to thrive in the area that requires deep thinking, analysis and scientific reasoning. Melancholy are not known to be a good leader because of their perfectionist attitude, their empathy and communication barrier, except when moderated by other temperaments. They are also reticent in accepting any new thing and are never drawn to things in vogue. They are inventors, writers, preachers, advertisers, architects, project managers, account executives, accountants, artists, fashion designers, on-air-personality, painting, drawing, and musicians. They are also drawn to analysis, evaluation and development in data processing and management, advanced medicine, software engineering and development, investigation, and artisan especially those that require a higher level of precision and constantly evolving.

Examples of Melancholy in the Bible are Abraham, John, David, Elijah, Isaiah, Daniel, Gideon, James, Mark, Deborah, Moses, Thomas, and Nathaniel.

Phlegmatic

Phlegmatic are those reserved, quiet and carefree. GOD made them that way because of a certain purpose HE wants to achieve. Person like Jacob, Moses, Joseph – the husband of the virgin Mary, Martyr, Nathaniel, Noah, Lot, Jonah. As you can see, this set of people is indispensable in birthing the kingdom of GOD. The only challenge with these people is that GOD had to do more than extraordinary, before they would finally surrender to follow their purpose. This is partly because they underestimate themselves, partly because they are obstinate and partly because they prefer certainty. They are a set of wonderful people who are consistent and faithful and with this positive attribute, they are more likely to build a cottage in a place they are supposed to erect a tent. They quickly set themselves down in the comfortable zone - comfort zone. Because of this, they are usually an underachiever. They're like tortoises and snails who hardly trust anyone other than themselves but when they do, they let down their guard.

There is no denying the fact that GOD used them mightily both in the Bible and now. You will find most of them as a teacher, a preacher, evangelists, bookkeepers, auditors, postmen, judges, police, librarians, warehousing, educational sector, civil service, firefighting, doctors, engineers, lecturers and artisans. They are mostly the best employee in most organizations but they are hardly recognized except with the long-serving employee award, so they are de jure employee of the year. They hate the spotlight but they're the unofficial backbone of the organization they work in.

Sanguine.

The father of Sanguine is Esau. Their carefree attitude makes them enjoyable to be with. If you happen to offend a sanguine, you just run away that moment, s/he will be begging you to come back. They thrive and are comfortable among people and they tend to be drawn to vocations that involve talking and uplifting people's spirit. If there's any temperament that quite easily achieves their destinies, it is this set. The reason that makes them succeed easily when others fail is their attitude to forgive easily especially, themselves. They don't dwell on failure and always set their face on the next thing. They live life on the speed lane and don't have time to waste thinking of what might go wrong. They are likely the first people to try new things and are always open to anything in vogue. They love meeting people; they love helping and can give everything they have. They tend to be drawn to creative industries that put them in the spotlight. Their strength is the people but they dread negative perceptions of others.

Esau was the father of Sanguine, Saul was another, Judah, Joseph, Aaron, Nehemiah, and Solomon. GOD loves this set of people because they don't harbour evil and forgive easily. They're strong candidates for unmerited favour.

Journalism, Teaching, Fashion, Creative industry, Sales and Marketing, Travel agent, Hotel, Real Estate, Entertainment, Painting, Interior Décor, and every job that grants spontaneity and meeting people are the forte of these people. They can also make a career in teen counselling as long as they guard themselves against temptation. Product review, online and digital marketing, dancer.

Choleric

Choleric are born leaders, David, Paul, Elisha, Peter, Samson, John the Baptist, and Joshua. They either commit all of themselves to something or none of themselves. They take decision fast and stick to it. They are drawn to military, politics, corporate governance, business, structural engineering, sales, law, talent management, accounting, investment banking, evangelism, public speaking, and strategy. They love the spotlight and can galvanize people towards a goal. They can be sadistic sometimes because they lack emotional intelligence. Detail and patience are not their strength but they can be workaholic and visionary. They see life as a competition, dog eats dog and are good at playing office politics.

GOD uses them a lot because they're very committed to what they believe in. When they believe in something; they're sold out to it. Anything that does not align with their interest does not attract their sympathy.

Why you should stick to your temperament

You naturally gravitate towards the vocation that your Temperament favours. It is counterproductive to covet a position where you won't naturally bloom. Many people are into vocation that they are not naturally gifted in and for this people, they put up a struggle to change from who they are to who the occasion demands. GOD did not make a mistake making you who you're; don't complicate things being who you are not.

There's no worse or better Temperament; we just have good or bad imitators.

Exercise:

Use the chart below; which of the 4 major temperament describes you?

Is what you are doing now, playing to your strength or not?

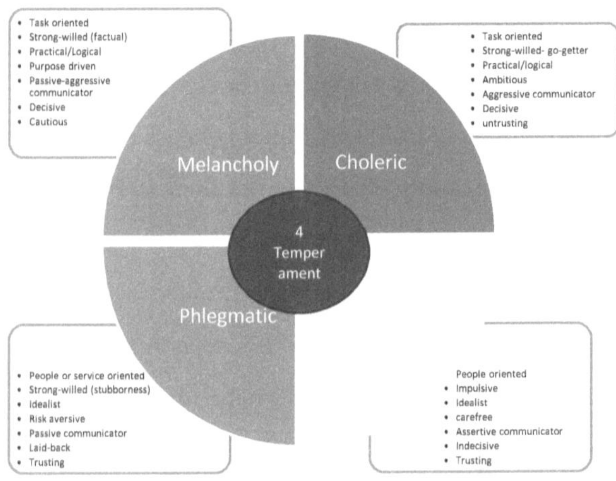

Temperament refers to inborn biologically based behavioral and emotional patterns that are observable in infancy and early childhood; Personality is the complex brew that emerges after cultural influence and personal experience are thrown into the mix.

Susan Cain

8

Your living Passion

Moses David, Joshua and Elisha's Experience

I often get confused when people talk about Passion. What most people call passion, is at best, hobby - what they like doing. It is like most people choose 'Passion' just to belong or get the feeling that they are not groping through the darkness of life. Passion has become a buzzword people throw around nowadays. It is like: the more fanciful your passion appears to be, the more person of substance you appear to be.

There's more to Passion than what people understand it to be. Passion is the unexplainable zeal that eats you up, the holy anger, the jealousy and an irresistible urge for a cause that is beyond you. Passion is not what you love, it is not a dream; Passion is the reason for your living; as basic and as important as life is, Passion is far more important.

Don't be stampeded into settling for anything as your passion, this marriage of convenience and it, would likely end in regret.

9 Litmus tests of PASSION

The only way to be sure that the thing you hold as your passion is truly what you claim it is, is by asking yourself these questions.

1.   <u>What is the Price?</u>

JESUS drove out those selling and buying in the Temple Jn 2: 13-17. This is the same JESUS that healed them, fed them, forgave their sins and would lay down HIS life for theirs. No diplomacy, no appealing, nothing; HE couldn't stand the temple being desecrated.

What you can negotiate for but not with it; what you can stoop low to have but you'd not stand that the thing be abused, then, that is your passion.

Ask yourself: Am I willing to pay **<u>any price</u>** to have that something but you'd **<u>not accept any price for that thing?</u>** JESUS negotiated and ransomed our lives with HIS life thus not willing to bargain with 'our soul' – the Temple.

Passion is the willingness to pay any price for something and the unwillingness to accept any price for the same thing Matt 13: 44.

2.   <u>Does it Rule You?</u>

In John 4, despite JESUS being weary and hungry, HE became enlivened, when HE met the Samaritan woman. Passion is like an intoxicant, a drive and opium that takes preeminence over your physical well-being. Passion rules not only your thoughts but also your actions. You don't say to Passion 'Wait, let me sleep, let me eat, let the sun go down or the rain stop Matt. 8: 22. Passion dictates to you; not conditions. Passion always acts like an emergency or a controlling force.

3. <u>What is greater than it?</u>

Moses became so zealous for Israelis that he killed an Egyptian brother and, in the process, blew up his cover. Passion and self-preservation are mutually exclusive most of the time. Moses knew he risked being found out but still did it anyway. David challenged a war veteran and a giant that held the whole nation to ransom for 40 days in the person of Goliath. David did not challenge Goliath because he was certain that he'd win but because he couldn't stand the mockery Daniel 3: 18.

Until the thought of losing your life becomes secondary to it; it is not yet a Passion. Passion makes you see self-preservation as a means to an end; your life means nothing without it. If you have to choose life over it, it is so you might have another chance at it.

4. <u>Do You Take it Personally?</u>

When Eliab, his brother threatened him in 1 Sam. 17: 29, David, snapped back at his brother, I know, it would have been an intense moment.

When you have Passion for something, you'd refuse to back down in the face of intimidation, temptation or prosecution even by the most important people in your life Lk 2: 49. If you cannot respectfully take a stand against your close family members for your

Call; if are still concerned about not losing face before family and friends and colleagues; what you have, my friend, is desire not Passion Matt. 10: 34 -39. Your friends, family love you so much that they would do everything within their power to impede you from going for what they can't see, unfortunate for everyone, no one except really understand what is set before you Matt. 16: 23.

5. <u>Is Anything too Big?</u>

Peter just caught the largest fish in the entire Samaria at that time. The catch would have made him the richest fisherman, yet; he abandoned all to follow after JESUS. Elisha slaughtered 24 cows at the time Israel was just coming out from severe famine. He abandoned his prosperous life to become a trainee. It is not only his status he abandoned; he also burnt the bridge back to his wonderful life. Killing the cows satisfies Mk.10: 17–22. He left without saying goodbye to his parent who would've tried to stop him from going Lk. 9: 62.

When there's something too big to sacrifice for Passion, it is not the Passion you have. Whatever you take as your Passion becomes all you've got. You either swim or sink with it.

6. <u>Does It Make Sense?</u>

Didn't it occurred to Elisha that he might never become a prophet because of the sheer numbers of the sons of prophets who were ahead of him in ranking? That didn't deter him from leaving his comfortable life to start all over again by becoming a student in Prophet Elijah's School of Ministry. It doesn't make sense for someone to leave a stable and prosperous life for a life of uncertainty and persecution.

When 'what if' does not become your albatross, when you're not so much concerned about failing, when you don't need assurance before committing yourself to something; then you may have what's called Passion. With Passion, you're not crippled by the thought of 'what if' but 'what is' or 'why'.

7. <u>Does It lose Its drive?</u>

Passion is a living force. Moses, probably became aware of his mandate when he was just a teenager or in his early twenties when he started developing this sympathy towards the Israelis' plight. By 30, this sympathy was beginning to eat him up. And at 40, this urge was so strong and so real that he killed an Egyptian without thinking.

When you observe the conservation between Moses and the Fire in the bush, you will notice that the Person (Fire in the bush), didn't have to convince Moses about his purpose but how to go about it. "***Who am I to go before Pharaoh and to save the people? Who shall I tell them their GOD is? I have tried it with one of them and he didn't believe me, how shall they believe me this time?***"

These're the kind of objections you'd expect from someone who's being tormented by the thought of something s/he cannot do anything about.

Even after 40 years in Midian, the passion didn't die. Moses never stopped having that burning desire but had to talk himself out of it all of the time by consoling himself that he tried but the people didn't want him.

What is that thing you saw yourself doing, 10, 20, 30 or 40 years ago that has not lost its meaning or appeal to you up till now? What is that possibility you have kept in the cooler of your potential? What is that thing you know you can always fall back on, even if everything else fails - your last card? That is where your Passion lies.

8. <u>Is it all about You?</u>

Passion is all about service while work is only about reward. You're not going into it because of what is in it for you. No. Even if there's 'nothing' in it for you, you'd still happily go for it because of the satisfaction you derive. GOD didn't tell Moses or anyone for that matter their gains or benefit for the roles HE's calling them into. GOD only told Moses that he'd be a god to Pharaoh, that should be enough reward for him.

Of the only 3 people who wanted to use their calling as a means of personal aggrandizement in the Bible, 2 of them didn't end well. You talk about Gehazi, you talk about Judas Iscariot.

This is how you'd know if what you have is a Passion or not. When you are fascinated about it because of pecuniary reason, status or ego, it is surely not a Passion.

9. <u>Passion is a Spirit</u>

GOD told Moses to anoint Joshua because he had the Spirit in him Num. 27: 18. GOD told Elijah to anoint Elisha (a farmer) in his stead. The choice of Elisha was not arbitrary as GOD was so detailed to the point of his daily itinerary. GOD saw something in him that HE didn't see in the sons of the prophets. Elisha's drive to be a Prophet was not borne out of the yearning of the heart not of personal ambition, it was not an aspiration, not for self-sake, not for the prestige. While the sons of the prophet saw it as work, Elisha saw it as his life calling; while the sons of the prophet saw it as an opportunity for wealth, he saw it as an opportunity for service.

One pertinent question to ask oneself is: what now happened to the sons of the Prophet?
Nothing. Absolutely nothing. They didn't become what they wanted and didn't amount to what GOD had made them for, either. They led a wasted and unimpactful life. One of them even used his two sons as surety to take a loan just to eat, 2 Kings 4. Even Gehazi who nearly became something, got his life mangled as the result of trying to belong to where his true longing isn't.

You can never fake Passion. If you don't have Passion for it, don't do it. GOD has so created you as a Precision tool for a Particular Purpose; you're only going to blunt out yourself struggling for what's someone else'. Doing something you don't have Passion for, means you'll always need to be cajoled and be incentivized to do it. You will never give your best to it while your best lies in ruin.

Elijah did not know anything about Elisha but GOD who knew him so much, ordered Elijah to anoint him as prophet in his stead. It didn't matter what Elijah thought about it, nor who he had prepped to be his successor; when GOD truly sees your heart, HE will fish you out from the most obscure place just like David.

Passion is a currency that buys what relationships can't.

Purpose ≠ hobby ≠ gift ≠ Dream ≠ Passion

The common misconception that has left numerous destinies derelict and crippled, is confusing hobby, gift, and dream to be one's Purpose. This is one major misinformation by the so-called life coaches and motivational speakers.

No one ever finds fulfillment at the bus stop of gifts, hobbies, or dreams.

Many gifted and talented individuals made a mess of their lives because they made their gift an end in itself when it is meant to be a means to an end.

Joseph was gifted with the gift of dream; his hobby was to interpret dreams and his dream (aspiration) was to be out of prison. Yet, his life's Purpose was far more than this. Jacob's desire in life was to inherit his father's dwindled estate Gen. 28: 21; he loved (hobby) cooking, and doing house chores Gen. 25: 27, but his Purpose in life was totally different from what he was becoming.

When you observe great men in the Bible, you see those, whose life's Purpose, are direct graduation of their hobbies, gifts, talents, dreams, example are Joseph and David; however, not a few others, found their Purpose in life, as a complete departure from where their lives were heading to, examples are Jacob, Elisha.

Someone said: *assumption is the mother of frustration*. Don't assume that because you love doing something and there is market for that, then, your Purpose in life lies there.

So, how to do discover your Passion and Purpose in life from your Dream, Gifts, Talents and Hobbies? Find out below.

5 Stages between Desire and Purpose and the Steps

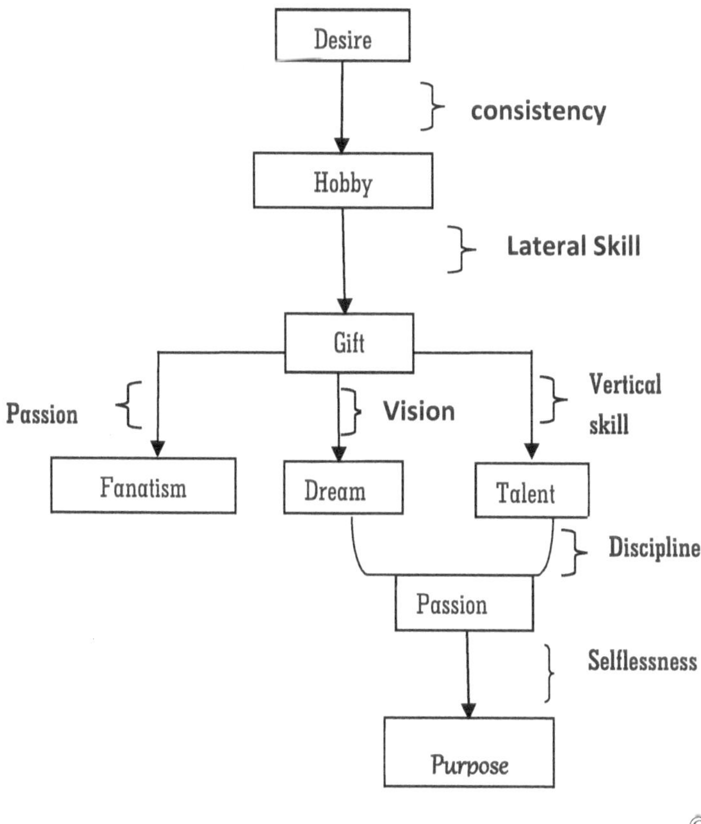

Desire

Let's start from the most basic of it all, your desire. What do you want to become in life? What is your life's ambition? Where do you see yourself in the next 10years? What do you want in life? What are your goals? These questions are as useless as their answers. They are, at best, useful at job interviews or for those who haven't figured out what to do with their life.

How can someone say his life ambition is to continue to learn and improve as a person? Do you want to be ever learning and never coming to understanding?

What happen to making one's life ambition to be who GOD has made one to be? What happens to telling oneself that in the next 5 years, I want to be able to speak this or that language so that I would be able to reach more soul for Christ or to show more people the basis for their life instead of them groping through the darkness of life? Instead of saying I want to be a better person; say I want to find out what person I am made to be and to become it?

Any aspiration that is not inspired from within can never be a life ambition; you are merely reacting or trying to blend with your surrounding like a chameleon.

You want to be a doctor because of the subtle power that they possess, even the President of a nation would dutifully obey his doctor's medication? You want to be a cloud engineer, business analyst, AI and machine learning expert because they are in vogue? What is the base of your desire? Is the foundation of your purpose worthwhile, would it stand any assault thrown at it even from hell?

I have no intention of discouraging you from aspiring; but, for self's sake, let your aspiration be in line with your inspiration? Learning skills in vogue should not be a life ambition but an ambition for life (your Purpose in life).

Why should you spend 20, 30, 50, 70 years or an eternity with the spur of the moment? If you are going to commit yourself to something, let it be something that is committed to you, then make that thing a hobby. Don't be tempted to believe that since it is your committed to you then you have it in the bag. No. You have to make a hobby out of it for the desire to yours.

Hobby

Hobby is not only how you relax. It is not only the little things that you do to restore your sapped energy and keep you motivated. A hobby is something you like to do without losing interest. Hobby is a consistent desire.

Naturally, hobby is not unique. You'd be one of the several million if not billions out there, who derive pleasure in similar things as you do, and relax and refresh same way.

Do you love reading? Millions do. Your hobby is to travel and meet people. Hundreds of Millions also.

If like several other millions, your Purpose is derived from that which is that pervasive, how do you have your uniqueness then? If you're like any other person out there, how can you say GOD tailor-made you, or if you're created at all?

You don't make your hobby your call; you make your call your hobby.

Hobby is too generic to be personal.

Instead of asking yourself 'what you love doing', ask what is most unique to you.

- Out of 10 people I know, how many people find my 'hobby' similarly interesting?

- To what degree do they find it engaging as I do?

- Do I derive satisfaction from complementary things?

Let's assume that you love reading; you cannot say because you love reading that you're called to be a writer:

Ask:

- In a random population, how unique is the interest to you? Let assume that over half of the people that you know loves reading too. This is a red flag.

- The next is to ask yourself: What's level of my interest compared to others? If out of the people that love reading, you're among the 10% that dedicate 2hr daily. It's still not yet unique to you.

- Does your commitment show more than just interest? Can you sacrifice your other needs in order to have more of that? When you don't have the time, do you create time for it by denying yourself certain physical needs? Do you inconvenience yourself to have more of it?

- What else do you do? Do you just read books and move on to the next one or do you create axillary interest from that? Does it catch your attention and also spur your creativity? Can you create 5 new books from a single book or do you just read to be entertained?

By the time you're done answering these questions, you will know if truly you have a Call out of your hobby or not.

Your hobby is nothing, too simple to make life out of. You need to move a step further to turn your hobby into a gift as Joseph did.

You must invest in that hobby by learning as much as possible about the hobby so that you will be skillful in it. You must develop lateral skill (be an expert in that hobby) to turn it into gift.

GIFT

This is where your real work begins. This is when you demonstrate your commitment to living for your Purpose or living for yourself. Most people failed to move past this level because they believe that: Gift is all that matters.

Gift is your God-given natural ability that opens you up to your purpose or that opens up your purpose to you.

Your gift may not be your purpose but it may pave the way.

Everyone knows how gifted Lionel Messi is when it comes to football. The guy is so gifted that he has won 8 FIFA World Player of the Year. Is football his Purpose?

I know this is a hard question for you to answer. But think about someone like great Pele. Pele retired from football at the age of thirty-seven but still went on to live till eighty-two years. If it football was his purpose, why didn't he die after retiring from it?

Understand that Joseph gift of dream interpretation was a very lucrative venture in those days, especially in Egypt. With that alone, Joseph could have set up a consultancy firm downtown Cairo, and his brothers would still have come and bowed before him.

But, was that his Purpose? No.

> I have seen many gifted and talented individual that went broke, sick and unimpactful, but I have never seen anyone who is living out the Purpose not impactful.

Of what impact is your gift if it is only to bring you profit? When you stop at the level of gift; you have abused the grace of GOD upon your life and you may end up being enslaved to it.

Imagine what would've happened had Joseph interpreted Pharaoh's dream without providing a solution.
Do you think someone would've managed the 7years of plenty and famine as well as Joseph did?
One thing I'm sure of, is this: Joseph wouldn't have died as nobody in Egypt. Jacob and his family could have died in Canaan, because, Joseph, who's supposed to bring them to Egypt to preserve, failed.

Fulfilling your destiny is not only for you. It acts as a launchpad for many destinies coming after you and for those tied to yours. This is why, I so much believe that: fulfilling your purpose is tantamount to bringing the kingdom of GOD down on this earth because you'd be working with GOD to actualize HIS cosmic plan. There may be no heaven for you if your life counts for nothing here on earth Revelation 21:8. You engaging in your purpose brings answers to some people's prayer.

Lazarus didn't have the smallest cottage in heaven but had to put up with Abraham because he led an empty, barren life. We understood with him because he was sick; what about you? what would your excuse be?
That you have a gift does not automatically translate you into Purpose. There are certain recipes you need to add in proper sequence before you can attain your Purpose here on earth. Let's take a look at different possibilities from Gift one after the other.

Fanatism

You can become a fanatic when you just add passion to your gift. When you impassion your gift without understanding what it is or seeing the big picture. Your Gift is just an infinitesimal aspect of the whole. When you take it as an end to itself, you've effectively cut it off from the cosmic plan Matt 19: 7 – 8.

Being a fanatic is a dead end on its own. You cannot discover your Purpose from fanatism unless you retrace your step back to reevaluate what you think you know about your gift 2 Pet. 1: 5. The way you'd know if you're being fanatic is to ask yourself if you have impassioned your gift. You'd know if nothing else matters to you aside the gift. If you use your gift to justify any form of inhumanity because of your belief or training, Paul was such a person before he met Christ.

You don't add passion to gifts but you can make passion out of your gifts.

Dream

I talked extensively on Dream in **3 Keys to Riches.** You'll do yourself a world of good if you grab a copy.

Until you understand what Dream is, you may not enjoy the richness of it.

DREAM is

> **D** = **D**rive
> **R** = **R**esponsibility
> **E** = **E**xpectation
> **A** = **A**spiration

M = **M**ap with which one navigates the world of many side attractions.

You can only move from Gift to Dream when you have a vision, i.e., an end, in mind. You don't just celebrate the gift; your gift must flow into something bigger, something purer than the gift itself. You must see beyond the gift into how the gift can birth your inspiration. You are a gifted singer; how'd that gift enable you to achieve what GOD shows you?

Dream is not taught, it is thought; it is not desired, it is discovered, it is not aspired, it is inspired; it is not what you conceive, but what you receive; not what you imagined, but what you uncovered; not fantasized but accepted; not what you want, but who you're.

Dream Equation

Dream = Desire + Consistency + Skill + Vision

Gift = Desire + Consistency + Skill (training)

Dream = Gift + Vision

<u>Talent</u>:

Talent is developing a level of expertise in different fields relating to your primary gift.

Gift brings you before kings, talent makes you stand before kings. You wouldn't want to kiss your breakthrough goodbye the day you see it, would you?

While dedicating yourself is enough for a gift, you need diligence to turn the gift into talent.

You don't just invest in the gift and expect to be celebrated; you must invest around the gift also.

Joseph turned his gift into talent by learning management, food preservation, data analysis, physics, chemistry, agriculture, and many more subjects while in slavery.

GOD didn't tell him what to learn, GOD just put him in an environment where he could learn. What excuse do you have?

Joseph understood that GOD didn't send him down to Egypt by mistake. He knew he'd have died from his brothers' hand but for GOD's intervention. He saw beyond his plight in Potiphar's house and in Prison. Joseph was made in the most difficult time of his life, his NIGHT time of life.

Imagine Joseph had interpreted Pharaoh's dream but did not give that unsolicited solution of storing grains in the time of plenty. Joseph had the gift of dream interpretation. His gift could only bring him before Pharaoh but it was his talent that made him to continue to stand before Pharaoh as the second in command.

Gift brings you to the threshold of destiny, but Purpose that ushers you into it.

Gift and Talent makes you to be influential; Purpose makes you rule.

Without seeing that your gift is just to bring you before your Pharaoh, you will miss out on your destiny.

Talented Musician

I have never heard of a gifted musician because Music has different aspects to it. You can have a gifted guitarist, a gifted drummer, or a gifted singer but you can only have a talented musician.

Your gift is the 'you' in your crude form. It needs refining and further development. As petroleum is useless in its crude form and thus commands lesser value, so your gift when not invested into. Don't just invest in your gift, invest around it also.

Lateral Vs. Vertical Skill Development

Lateral(horizontal) is subject matter, specialist training, vocational tied and restrictive expertise. Lateral skill development makes you to be an expert in a certain human endeavor. You are so dedicated to that your hobby that you make a it a gift. You are sold out to it. Vertical skill development is about adaptiveness, it is about being diligence, going beyond the sky, seeing beyond your current scope and developing yourself along multifront. You don't just limit yourself to your task, you also adjoin yourself to relevant tasks in such a way that the task is sold out to you.

JOHN the Baptist; the bad workman 2 Tim 2: 15.

John the Baptist was gifted uniquely but boxed himself into a small box of the crude form of his gift. John didn't invest in

You can be gifted and be cheated out of a position; but you cannot be talented and be rejected.

himself. He used to pray, he used to fast but lacked knowledge. He didn't study to show himself approved. No wonder the least in the kingdom (those working their garden) is greater than him Matt 11: 11. He even had the temerity to question if JESUS was the Messiah!

He was ignorant.

John restricted himself to his gift alone, i.e., to baptize. He knew his calling was to be precursor to JESUS yet, he did not deem it necessary to know better than everyone else, about the Person he was supposed to witness for. He did not even know much about himself, let alone Christ John 1: 21 and Matt. 17: 12 – 13.

When you lack knowledge, no gift will speak for you while your head is being chopped off with the dance of one small damsel Mt. 14:10.

You need knowledge in the form of either vision or vertical skill development to take your gift beyond the realm of fanatism.

Passion

Both dream and talent can metamorphose into passion if the carrier is disciplined enough.

Dreams and Talent are under your control. You can decide how you use your Talent, but not your Passion. Passion controls you.

You need a great dose of discipline to be able to subject your convenience and comfort under something you can call off its bluff.

Passion is not how you feel but what you are.

PURPOSE

Passion is good but not enough to constitute your Purpose if it is not selfless. What makes work a Purpose is the expectation of appreciation or reward. If you expect reward from others, you'd be so disappointed. You have been fully compensated for by the one who engages you. Matt. 6: 31 - 33. Every other compensation is merely an addition.

Exercise:

Try to take your plan, ambition or goal in life through the 5 stages between desire and purpose; and see if you would be able to find your way through the maze; use the steps enumerated as a guide.

I had a new sense of purpose, and it had nothing to do with my recognition and exploit on a bike. Some people won't understand this, but I no longer felt that it was my role in life to be a cyclist. Maybe my role was to be a cancer survivor. My strongest connections and feelings were with people who were fighting cancer and asking the same question I was: 'Am I going to die?'

Lance Armstrong

9

Your Experience

Abraham, David, Joseph, Samuel, Moses, Jacob, The Apostles

What's cognate about the experience of Moses' shepherding goats, cows and sheep; to delivering the Israelites from bondage in Egypt? That Peter, who had been destined to be the righthand man of the Messiah, was nothing but a fisherman is nothing short of fascinating. What happened to being a priest or a politician?

For 40 days Goliath taunted the Israelites; the people that were trained in the act of warfare couldn't take up Goliath's gauntlet; it took one small Shepherd boy who couldn't even wield a sword nor wear armor to restore the nation's pride.

The Palestines were not stupid to put their hope in an ordinary warrior. Goliath was more than a warrior, he had proven to be unkillable with arrow, bow, sword, and other conventional weapons, that's why his people could go as far as telling the Israelites that if the Israelites could kill him, they and their children would become their slave forever 1Sam. 17:9.

It seemed that it's Saul and Israel that was the 'stupid'. Putting their hope in a rookie, is nothing but preposterous. I am sure that Saul did so either to buy time or to get David, an irritant, out of the way.

What they didn't know was that while Goliath was training himself to be immune to anything made of iron, GOD was training

David in unconventional weapons like using ordinary stone and rubber to fight war. It looked as if David was forgotten in the bush, but it was GOD that engaged him as HIS trump card against Goliath.

Do you believe that everything works together for good to those who answer to GOD's purpose?

As long as you're alive, everything happening in your life is GOD teleguiding you to an end only HE sees.

It means to say, that every of your experiences that is not attributable to sin is according to the Purpose GOD has for you.

How to Factor Your Purpose from Your Experience

There are 4 possible ways you can factor out your Purpose from the happenings in your life that you call, your Experience.

You can use the Lowest Common Multiple (LCM), Lowest Common Factor (LCF), or Highest Common Factor (HCF) and Matrix.

Lowest Common Multiple (LCM)

Mathematically, LCM is the multiple of all the events. It is a unique value that each value tends to, in different multiples.

Assume these numbers: 1, 2, 3, 4, 5, 6, 10, 12, 15, 20, 30 and 60. The only thing all of them have in common is 60. Each of them is 60 in different multiples. 1 in 60 times is 60. 2 makes 60 on the 30th turn. 12 every day makes 60 in 5 days, while 20 in each year for 3 years turn 60.

You borrow a leaf from this principle to decipher your purpose. Look at the events in your life so far, can you see where your life is leading you to? Is your life aligning perfectly towards an end?

Look at Samuel, a classic example. He was born a prophet, he lived a prophet, and died as one. He was defined and commissioned at birth by GOD, so no need for him to discover any Purpose, his purpose has found him out. Samson, John the Baptist are other credible examples.

Steve Jobs, Stephen Wozniak, Micheal Jackson, Lionel Messi, Whitney Houston, Mark Zuckerberg, Thomas Edison, Aristotle, Bill Gates, Chiamanda Adiche, Oprah Winfrey, Morgan Freeman, Kobe Bryant, the Williams sisters, Adele Blue Adkins, Tiger Woods all have their Purposes right lined up in a single file. Most of them started when they were as early as 2, or 3 years of age. They are called gifted, child prodigies, and so on.

For some, their purpose is that thing they were born into, while for some, what they were born into leads them to their purpose. Take for example Steve Jobs. Almost everything about him narrowed and set him up for who he'd eventually become. His life followed a single pattern. He was adopted into a technology-savvy family. His adoptive father was a machinist. He loved electronics and humanities while growing up. He could dismantle and fix any gadget. His first job was at Atari Corporation as a video game designer at 19 years of age. His trip to India spurred his mantra of affordable quality, his meeting with Stephen Wozniak with the two sharpening each other in achieving their mandates, his adopted parent's financial tightness made him think long and hard and cut down on frivolities, his days at Reed College where he learnt calligraphy which birth stylish fonts. Steve Jobs wasn't just an inventor but an inventor with artistic flair. Everything about him made a specific man that made it possible to have a personal computer that is sleeky, light, sturdy, and user-friendly.

Your Purpose is as old as you're, if not older. It has always been with you; not something you pick along the way.

You have to go down memory lane and walk you path to the presence. Do you see a consistent track you walked all through your life? If so, it is likely leading you to your destiny.

Highest Common Factor (HCF)

There're instances that your life and your experience gravitate you towards your purpose. In such a situation, you'd not see a rigid similarity or a clear-cut pattern of consistency in your life. Your life may look like: of -8, -16, 28, -32, 40. It is not easy to spot a pattern here. You can say there's a connection but no consistency. You don't have experience in a single or similar line of vocation; you're the jack of all trades; master of none.

Abraham's life follows this pattern. He didn't settle in a place, or a vocation for most of his life. At Ur (Iraq), he was skilled in crafting images; a skill he picked from Terah his idol-making father. He became a Prophet for a few years when he ran to Noah his great-grandfather; he learned salesmanship after returning to Ur and selling his father's artifact. At Haran (Turkey), he was a tent maker, where he also picked up an interest in raising cattle. Just when he was beginning to find stability, GOD told him to leave everything and go to Canaan. On getting to Canaan, the place didn't look like where he would love to stay for long, so he moved to the east of Bethel before moving southwards and finally landing in Egypt. Abraham was both a wanderer and a jack of all trades Deut. 26: 5. Drifting from one place to another without settling down.

Take Moses as another example. Moses was born an Israeli but raised as an Egyptian. He was trained as an administrator but got his first job as a soldier. He was also an engineer before becoming a shepherd, in Jethro and Daughters Diary farm; and finally, an oracle of GOD. There's nothing like consistency in Moses' life.

Who else could have led the people out of Egypt than he who understood the nitty gritty about Egypt and their god? His many experiences gave him knowledge of the workings of Egyptian military tactics and the bureaucracy. Being a fugitive taught him survival skills, and being a shepherd gave him the temperament to lead people of varying characters.

Talk about Jeff Bezos, Lance Armstrong, Tom Bradley, Nelson Mandela, and Mahatma Gandhi, most of them found their purpose out of their meaningless and unstable lives Jer. 29: 11. If all these people could later find Purpose, you have hope.

Look at the numbers -8, -16, 28, -32, 40 again, can see the pattern now? You won't if you can't see beyond the outcome.

-8 = 2*2*-2

-16 = 2*2*-2*2

28 = 2*2*7

-36 = 2*2*3*3*-1

40 = 2*2*2*5

$$\underline{2}*\underline{2} = 4$$

You need to do similar thing to your life if you want to know what the future wants you to hold onto. Stop sensationalizing the events in your life and you'd be able to see through the opaqueness. When you are fixated on failure, you lose out on what GOD wants to do. Always remember that GOD is not a sadist Matt. 7: 9: 11. That you ask for food and GOD sends you rain means GOD wants you to be a sower not an eater because HE has seen into your future.

You can factor your Purpose from your experience.

You were once a marketer, a clerk, a warehouse personnel. You studied science-related courses at college; I will not be surprised if your calling is Consultancy, Counselling, or Business analysis. Surprised?

This is the beauty of HCF. You may or may never know what you will discover when you follow your absolute experience.

Lowest Common Factor (LCF)

What if your life experience is not leading you nor gliding you towards a clear end, does it now mean you don't have a calling? What if your life's experience doesn't follow any smooth pattern, just a pile of mess that you cannot make any sense of? What if like Jacob, your experience has taken you from being in the kitchen to being on the farm, two parallel worlds that cannot be reconciled? You look at your life, there's no connection nor consistency among your experience so far; what do you do? How do you factor out what you're supposed to do to make your life fulfilling?

Jacob felt that way also Gen. 28: 20 – 21. He could not see what to make out of his life after 80 years of being on earth.

David, a shepherd, a singer, and a warrior. There's no connection among these professions, yet, he became the king.

Don't be too quick to dispose all your 'nonsense', GOD could mold a new you from it.

My Bible told me that, we really don't have anything except what we have been given 1 Cor. 4: 7, 1 Pet. 4: 10. From the foregoing, it is safe to say that it is wrong to say 'I make a mistake or it is a mistake'. Whenever we are saying it is a mistake, we are also indicting GOD of 'misgive'. Can GOD ever mis-? No. except we take something that we are not given, there's no mistake.

Every disjointedness and malalignment in experience is exactly the right mix for the next king after Saul.

As a shepherd boy, he proved that he would not abandon the sheep (people) even in the face of danger to his own life. As a singer, he showed that no matter what he became, he'd always glorify GOD. As a warrior, he demonstrated uncommon courage that Saul lacked. He showed that he could always galvanize the people 1Sam.17: 52.

Jacob's Purpose was to birth the ladder (JESUS) that would reconnect man to GOD yet Jacob had some negative characters that must be destroyed before stepping into his Purpose. This is why GOD took him through certain unpalatable experiences to break him down and remold Israel from the old Jacob.

When you look at your life and you cannot see a clear path,

you're just making motion no movement; it might be there's one soft skill, a virtue that is so, germane, to your functioning in your calling that you lack; until you learn it, you won't be able to step into your Purpose.

You cannot be ruled by fear, hatred, ego, impatience, indiscipline, jealousy, avarice, and think you'd fulfill your mandate here on earth.

You also can filter out your Purpose from your experience. You just need to revisit the major events in your life, examine what skill or important life lesson you learnt from them. What is that important thing GOD took you those experiences to work on? Is it confidence? Is it your work ethic? Is it your patience? Is it humility? Now, consider where that skill is a prerequisite; that is your Calling. GOD made you to learn the skill(s) because they are important for the assignment HE has for you.

Matrix

You also can know your divine mandate when for no reason opposition rises against you for attempting to do something.

If there's anything people easily agree to is something that is against the Will of GOD because you can't serve Mormon and serve GOD. Friendship with this world is an enmity with GOD.

When you have an idea and people vehemently oppose that idea not because it contravenes any law or natural justice system, then the idea is most likely from GOD.

Another way you can use this Matrix is to flip to the other side of what the world wants you to believe. It is not only your idea the world would try to attack but sometimes it is you.

Let's assume that people always misunderstand your intention or people twist your words always. This might be pointing you that you're the new Moses. That you're to lead the people to freedom from slavery. You can be a writer, a speaker, an evangelist, a political leader, and so on.

If your challenge is that people always pay you back bad for good like Joseph, your calling might be generational preservation. You must not stop doing good otherwise, you become irrelevant

If people discount you or never reckon with you, GOD might be preparing you to be the greatest king just like David. When you're undervalued, never you accept their valuation, and don't fight with them either.

It is time to gather your dossier and flip through the pages of your life, look for the salient message, the consistent information your life is revealing. There is something there you need to move into your future; if not, you would remain on the same spot.

There's an African proverb that says: when a child falls, the child looks ahead; but when an elder falls, the elder looks behind.

You are an elder, you have to take stock of your life to discover yourself.

Exercise:

List your experience over the last couple of years that constitutes two-thirds of your years so far, using the equation described in this chapter, what can you say your life is leading to?

Experience is what you get when you don't get what you wanted
Randy Pausch

The past is always around to hurt the future of those who deify it and of those who disregard it.

What an elder sees sitting down; a child may not see climbing the highest mountain
African Proverb

My brethren, count it all joy when you fall into various trials, knowing that the testing of your faith produces patience. But let patience have its perfect work, that you may be perfect and complete, lacking nothing.
Jm. 1: 2 -4

10

The Call

The call of GOD on Moses was as spectacular as what you and many people may be going through today.

You just lost your job unjustly? Don't ask GOD why me, but ask, what's next. Discuss with HIM, perhaps, you were too busy to hear HIS call, that incident is to get your attention.

If you study the events surrounding Saul's journey, you will see element of Divine influence. He was right in the thick of GOD's plan for his life. GOD orchestrated the not-so-palatable happenings: the loss of sheep, the search, the choice of the servant, and the coming of Samuel to Zuph, just to make him have a date with destiny.

If you were Moses, you walked kilometers to find pasture for your beleaguered herd without success, someone told you that there's the pasture on the other side of the wilderness, only to get there and find the pasture on fire: what would you do?

Unlike what most of us would do, Moses saw beyond what was visible. It was so apparent that the pasture was on fire yet Moses turned aside to see. When he turned aside, he saw something beyond the natural in his predicament. He saw that the bush was not consumed. The ability to see while crying gave Moses an encounter with destiny.

Our immediate reaction to jeopardy would either open us up to the invisible or shut us up in the mundaneness of life.

When GOD called Samuel, he mistook GOD's voice for Eli's voice. We can forgive him for that because of his age, he was barely 12 years old at that time but what are your excuses? You're going about looking for who's responsible for the misfortune happening to you. You have blamed it on your colleague, your parents, your spouse, and so on, and now, you're running out of who else to blame, you now blame it on the devil. Haba.

Maybe, all these misfortunes happening to you are the result of ignoring GOD and HE is using it to get your attention.

For many people, GOD has been telling them their Purpose here on earth but they have consistently resisted the call. To them, they want GOD to convince them before they can leave that plumb job before they leave their comfort zone and foray into the unknown.

My question to you at this moment is: are you sure of what you're asking for?

If something, like what happened to Paul, like what happened to Joseph, like what happened to Balaam, like what happened to Moses and Jonah; happened to you, would you still be standing?

Let me tell this disturbing truth. Before GOD would call you in a dramatic fashion that you crave, a lot of things would have gone wrong. If you don't believe me, ask Moses what happened to him between the period of 10th year and 40th year in Midian.

This also coincides with the most brutal years for the Israelis in Egypt. This was when the burden was so great that even GOD couldn't sit on the throne peaceably because of their everyday groaning.

As the people were groaning, Moses' life was floundering. He was poor, weak, sickly, and dishonoured by his wife and her family.

The Bible does not tell us much about that but the fact that Moses had to travel to the other side of the wilderness to look for pasture for his father's in-law herd was not by his own volition. He did that because his life depended on those cattle. The cattle are more valuable to Jethro than Moses' life.

When things are not going well with you and you have done everything right, instead of looking around for the answer, look unto GOD. Ask yourself in what way you have chosen your ego over GOD's Purpose.

We have seen many people who discovered their Purpose from breakthroughs, we have also seen others who discovered their purpose after failures.

Be a Purpose-driven person, not a success-seeking individual.

> Success is not final; failure is not fatal; Purpose is the ultimate.
>
> Success outside of one's Purpose is a failure in disguise.

Don't admire the characters in the Bible or vilify them until you put yourself into their shoe. King Saul was this close to frustrating his breakthrough and ascension to the throne had he allow the loss of the cattle to make him take offence in GOD like what most

Christians do these days. Saul had that encounter with Samuel because he judged GOD faithful even in his tragedy.

Exercise:

Look at the tragedy or loss in your life so far; which of them you cannot attribute to Satan?

In what ways are you replaying Jonah's script again in your life?

Is there an agelong desire of yours that you have repeatedly denied commitment?

What right do you have to reject any experience when you don't know your purpose yet?

II

Your Gut Feeling

Adam, Hezekiah, the Shunamite woman, Daniel, the 3 Hebrew boys.

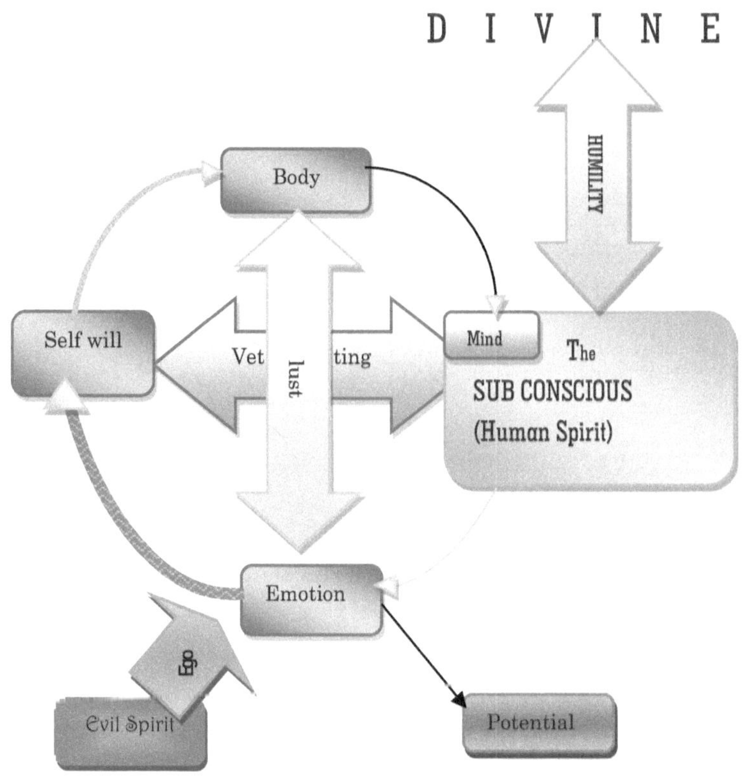

Human being is not just like other creatures; it's a living vessel that carries GOD and HIS capability. This happened when GOD breathed into Adam. Until GOD breathed into Man, Man didn't become. It is HIS breath that makes us be in HIS image Job 32: 8, not our physical structure.

Look at the representation above, it denotes that Humility is what makes us know the Will of GOD. As long as you're humble, you will be able to draw out wisdom from the Divine, through Gut feeling, Intuition, or Insight.

Humility is not just self-effacing but making yourself no more important than what GOD's purpose is. You are not humble if you cannot follow your heart. Humility is about having no other god aside from GOD. If because of what people would think or because of fear of what might happen; you'd not go after the reason GOD created you to fulfill it; just know that you've made gods out of these people and your ego.

What is a gut feeling and why you can trust it?

What is gut feeling?

Before we explore what gut feeling is, let's begin by exploring what gut feeling is not.

Number one is that gut feeling is not an instinct. An instinct is how you are wired genetically. It is a behavior passed down through generations to enable you to survive environmental exigencies. Most members of the species behave the same way because it is hard-wired in everyone within the population.

Secondly, gut feeling is not emotion. Any feeling that has a trace of fear, anger, hatred, jealousy, ego, self-serving, arrogance and so on, can never be from gut feeling. Before you can call your feeling an Intuition or gut feeling, it must not have a dab of emotion.

Thirdly, the Gut feeling is not temperament. It is quite easy to confuse your temperamental feelings with your gut feeling. Take for example your disposition towards risk; if you don't examine it properly, you may assume that feeling of yours is GOD speaking to you when in fact it is your temperament playing its charm on you.

Lastly, gut feeling is neither a learned nor conditioned behavior. Some people because of the experience have developed a template of reaction or feelings to certain occurrences, these feelings have become embedded in them that they usually believe they are coming from gut feeling. Some people have biases that are latent in them and these biases have a way of seeping through inside their thought process and fronting self as a gut feeling.

Characteristics of Intuition

I.   For the most part, Intuition is not reactive but creative. It is usually not in response to a situation but an insight into what is possible yet unthought of 1 Cor. 2: 9 – 10. The number criterion to use to analyze your feeling is if it is in response to something or if it is an idea that is new or impossible to think out by yourself.

II.   Intuition is from the part of the heart that is pure, quiet and selfless. When the feeling comes from the part of your heart that is not your selfish self, not your fearful self, not your egoistic self nor your wise self; when the source is not from the seat of reasoning nor from where hatred, lust, jealousy, ego, fear and so on usually emanate from. If it is the feeling that you'd not naturally agree to nor one that you can reason out.

III.   If it is not a reasonable decision to take. Know this for a fact, GOD would not speak to you through Intuition what you should know by wisdom or reasoning. If GOD is telling you to do something, it is probably because you cannot know the rightness by mere human intelligence. Intuition is GOD linking you up with something higher than what is available here on earth to heavenly wisdom.

IV.   Intuition is peaceful and calming. One strange thing about Intuition or gut feeling is that despite asking you to do what is unusual or uncommon (not sinful by the way), is that peace of mind or calmness it gives. Intuition would never tell you to do anything disgraceful but something that is both honourable and unheard of. After doing as bided, you immediately feel relieved. It feels like a mountain was taken off your shoulder.

V.   Another way to know if your feeling is an Intuition is that even your mentor (academic or spiritual) may not be able to agree with you but they would not be able to disagree with you on it. They will not be able to disagree with you because it doesn't contravene any law, precept or any good intentions, however, they may not be able to agree with you because it is an ethereal whisper into your heart.

VI.   Gut feeling is more pronounced when you are at the place of your Call, when your spiritual antenna is heightened as a result of prayer, fasting and worship.

You must dissect your feelings accurately so that you don't misjudge other feelings as Intuition. The difficult aspect of the work is to be aware of this possibility. Like they say, a problem well defined is half solved. You are now made aware that it is not all feelings from inside of you that is gut feelings. You can now see that some feelings are instinct, some are emotion, some are temperament and some are learned or conditioned behavior.

All you need to do is always situate your feelings against the discussed parameters.

Benefit of Intuition

Most discoveries and inventions we have today, even, from the worst of atheists, are the product of intuition. Intellect is limited, it studies what Intuition discloses. Intellect by design cannot discover new things. If it could, Albert Einstein, Steve Hawking, Isaac Newton and other inventors were not the most intelligent of their time their ideas were mostly criticized and fiercely opposed by scholars of their time. These scholars were experts, professors and celebrated academicians, yet, they did not see with their intellect what the inventors saw with their minds. This shows that intellect is a slave to intuition or let me put it in Mr. Einstein words:

The intuitive mind is a sacred gift and the rational mind is a faithful servant."

Exercise:

Aside from the 4 ways to make your gut feeling clearer, can you name 2 more ways?

What aspect of life do you expect GOD to speak to you intuitively?

What do you do if you can't feel anything in your gut?

The kingdom of heaven is within you, and whosoever shall know himself shall find it.

Egyptian proverb

It is through science that we prove, but through intuition that we discover.

Henri Poincare

There is no logical way to the discovery of these elemental laws. There is only the way of intuition, which is helped by a feeling for the order lying behind the appearance.

Albert Einstein

"I believe in intuition and inspiration…At times I feel certain I am right while not knowing the reason."

Albert Einstein

12

Your Thought

Mary, Zacharias and Moses

Thinking is the discussion that goes on within oneself. It is brainstorming with a sage within you.

One of the most awesome things about Thinking is the belief in the ability of the inside self to know everything, even things beyond the conjecture of 'outward self'. Sometimes, we even attempt to preempt the future or what is happening far away from us as it is happening. We all know or behave like we know that our soul knows far more than our head.

Why is that so?

Thinking, Daydreaming and Intuition

As easy, costless and priceless as thinking is, not everyone thinks. Thinking is not the thought that strays on in your mind; thinking is engaging in dispassionate discussion with the inner self (man). It is an intentional discussion aimed to produce a course of action.

Your thought is not your bedroom but a closet. You Don't live inside your head; think inside of it.

When your thinking process swerves from probing for solution to imagining the glory; when the object of your thinking is no longer how (strategy) but what it would be like (celebration); when you hold everyone and everything constant; when you have started counting your chicks before they are hatched, then, that process has left the realm of thinking to wishful thinking.

It is very easy to sink into that realm; but with discipline and thoughtfulness, you can always jolt yourself back to the task at hand Phil. 2: 5 – 11, Heb. 12: 2.

Think the process; see the outcome.

Thinking is not against GOD Lk. 14: 28. When Paul admonished us to renew our mind in Rom. 12: 2, he meant just that. Paul did not tell us to remove or renounce our mind, rather, Paul is telling us to continually update our mind. A book like this is a veritable means of doing so.

You cannot know the Will of GOD for your life without some element of thinking Josh. 1: 8. Thinking is a two-fold phenomenon. You think to know 'what' and you think to know 'how' and it is spiritual.

The physical Thinking also called worrying, reasoning rationalizing etc., can have a debilitating effect on the person. When you think physically, your brain is involved. If you put your brain under a scan, you would see that it is fired up the brain with some hormone, before you know it, you start feeling headache. This is the Thinking Jesus frowned against in Matt. 6: 25, the physical aspect of thinking (worrying).

There is a Spiritual aspect that has nothing to do with your intellect or your cap-ability (physical cap on ability) at all. You are

IF GOD DOES NOT GIVE YOU AN IDEA TO WORK ON BUT YOU BELIEVE YOU CAN FAITH YOUR DESIRE TO LIFE, YOU'RE JOKING

probing something beyond your current physical ability. In this kind of thinking, you don't make use of your brain but your mind. You don't rationalize it or thought about what you think is possible. It is not about what you see or hear, it is not what others are running after but that kingdom of GOD (purpose) within you.

You would know if you are using your head or your mind if the object of your thought is about what you want or what you covet in people. You would also know if it is your head or your mind if after sometimes, you start feeling headache or stress. The truth is that, you can stay probing on the GOD's plan for you for hours without it impacting on your health.

Yes. You may need to take a break. The reason for this is because your obtuse mind cannot fully grasp what GOD is telling you at the moment. Physically you are not stress but what you are thinking is just too much for your understanding or fathoming.

So, in real sense, Thinking is a spiritual exercise that Man use to connect to the unsearchable wisdom of GOD.

When you think, you think of 'what', 'who', 'when' and 'how'. You are not trying to rationalize the workability of 'what' but you want to know 'how'. Exo. 4: 10, Lk 1: 18 & 34.

You think Mary's way not Moses' nor Zacharias' way. You think to know what to do to make the 'what' to come to pass. You don't just hear what GOD is saying and now try to work it out by humanness. When GOD tells you 'What' ask HIM 'how'. Don't assume. Had Mary assumed that the message of the angel was a license for her and Joseph to copulate, the Messiah would not have come through her. Abraham met Sarah after the angel delivered the message when he was 99years because, that's how GOD wanted it.

Thinking is like drilling for Crude oil

There are 8 important stages of Crude Oil drilling and each of these stages are specific to the process of thinking out the Will of GOD.

1. Survey

It is not in every land you scout for Crude Oil, even though the Kingdom of GOD lies in your heart; you cannot discover it anyhow. This, unlike scouting for water which only requires you to do only electromagnetic survey or make use of your expertise, prospecting for Crude Oil does not lend itself to that. There are certain surveys you must carry out. You got to perform at least: the electromagnetic survey (people's opinion), the geological survey (covetousness), geochemical prospecting (lust), remote sensing (fear), gravimetry (Pride), magnetometry (capability), magnetotellurics (selfishness) and seismic survey (Anger). Until positive results are gotten from these tests, no further action is taken.

2. Data Analysis

The most critical step in performing these tests is done at the office not on the field. The data collected from these tests are then brought to the office and analyzed to truly hear the message behinds those statistics. The same thing you do after being told something, you have to go back to your closet (not your bedroom), to think on these data and ask GOD for guidance. Ask HIM, what is the message in it for you James 1: 21 – 24. You don't ask like Moses did just to get an excuse, you don't ask like Zacharias because you don't look it; you ask like Mary because you want to know what to do.

3. Surface Drilling

After the positive feedback is gotten from these studies, drilling begins. The first phase of drilling is to drill beyond the aquifer level which is about 100 to 200 feet below the ground. Moving past this level is one of the most difficult parts of the whole process. In fact, 90% of those that were able to go past stage 1 and 2 would not make it pass this level.

At this level, many people would quit because they are 'rewarded' too early for their dedication. They are not disciplined enough for delay gratification. They see water and their run riot on many things they can do. They now have water to drink, bathe, wash and even sell for money. They become like the big boy in their area, especially in areas where water is scarce.

You start seeing those you derive motivation from, your mentor and teachers quitting by the wayside. They have found something valuable even though it is not what they really wanted, but it kind of meet their needs.

Water is life

For you to move pass this level, you need to do a lot of insulation from the environment. You need to perform what is known as 'casing' to prevent your environment from contaminating your resolve.

You are scouting for oil not water, that is why you must always see the big picture. Generating Ideas at this depth is not the right zone to stay. You must dig deeper into you. You must drill through Ideas and your knowhow until you drill past it into a level way beyond your capacity, way beyond your reasoning capability.

4. Drilling into the Pay zone

There is a level, way beyond, what your reasoning and mental faculty can burrow into. A level that is cut off from the visible or your mental capacity. The aquifer zone is what knowledge or training can afford you, the pay zone is beyond the level of reasoning and rationing. It takes deep level of thinking to connect to that unsearchable depth of wisdom.

This zone is from 6000feet to over 15000feet deeper than the less than 200 level aquifer level. There is no level of reasoning you can do that would open you up to this level. Your brain is not fashioned for this level of efficiency, it is going to overheat and breakdown. Our brain's best is the aquifer level of life. Beyond this level into the pay zone (proven reserve) we need our Mind. We need a level of thinking that would persistently tarry with GOD for hours without burning out.

Drilling through to this level is not for the faint-hearted but faith-hardened. Imagine drilling with friends, colleagues, mentors, teachers and those that have been a source of encouragement to you stopped at a little just over 100 feet into the process because, they got a Greek gift - clean and clear water. It is not easy getting clean water around there, so, they were happy and done. Everyone packs up their drilling machine, install borehole and start selling water and also use the water for other socio-economic needs.

It takes much to have that courage to continue. You thank GOD for the water, but it is not what you saw in step 1 and 2. You need the water but you want something more. With the crude oil, you can buy up the area.

Let me be sincere with you. Do you know that after continuing to drill pass the aquifer level, you would stop seeing reward or result? I mean, you would have drilled pass the water, so, what you would continually encounter would be sand, rocks, mud? This is so scary. This is what everyone that finds purpose in life has to put up with. You can imagine the shame, the taunting, the loneliness, the pressure, the time, the rejection, the fear, the regret and so on. To make it more real, you are still searching for that 'reward' long after these people have settled on in life.

At this period in your life, you need the Lord's Prayer. You need a good dose of your daily bread just as Elijah, so that you don't faint on the way but strengthened to drill through to the trove of abundance. The daily bread here has nothing to do with food, because, Man shall not live by bread alone; the daily bread is the word of GOD that is telling you to drill on. The fortitude to persist.

5. Logging

Crude oil is only flows through the rig; it is not the rig that produces the Crude. Down there in the earth's crust, about 6000 – 15000 feet below the surface, there, the reservoir of Oil is. Until you diligently and patiently tarry in the place of 'thinking'; you cannot connect to the reservoir of wisdom inside of you.

That mean to say, what you need is relationship with GOD. Prayer, thanksgiving, sacrifice etc., have their importance, but the fundamental to keep the Well flowing is a relationship or connection to the wealth within and that is not possible without humility. You borrow down, you humble yourself, and take yourself of not more important than the word of GOD. The crude oil is not blue toothed (transferred wirelessly) from the reserve but flows through the rigs, in the same vein, you must let down yourself (be humble) to connect to the riches in GOD.

6. Wiper plugging

This is also an important step in Oil and Gas prospecting. It involves cleaning the inside of the rig of all debris and contaminants. You must consistently examine yourself. Look out for possible contaminant like ego, like fear, like hatred and lust. Even in 'humility', these 'things' have a way of seeping into if your mind is not continually renewed.

7. Fracking

Even after drilling into the **Pay Zone**, you still have some things to do before the oil starts running through the rig to the wellhead at the surface. This is called fracking. It is a method of injecting high-pressurized liquid or compressed natural gas to break through the rock formation that holds the reserve. Any Insight you get from thinking alone is just the specimen for you to take to the lab for a test. After some times, Inspiration would stop flowing. Fracking or adding proppant would break the fissures and keep it open; your prayer, speaking in tongue, worshiping and thanksgiving (monetary or otherwise) performs this same role. They act as proppants that keep the fissures open and grant you access to the inexhaustible riches in GOD.

8. Completing the Well

This involves everything you see on the surface. It involves laying the pipes, doing the electrical, mechanical, the pad, the safety and other works. The final step in the mining process.

The Thinking process you embarked upon is to know what to do. Now that GOD has shown it to you, you must go ahead and act accordingly.

You have responsibility to see to it that you act most intelligently according to what GOD shows you. This is where diligent comes to play. You must do your part and make other parts do their parts. Afterall, it is your life and you owe it to yourself to see that you create market for your crude oil otherwise you would be termed a fool.

Exercise:

How do you know the thought of your heart is from GOD?

What is the difference between thinking with your brain and in your mind?

What do you think cause people not to become what GOD has made them to be?

Our world is shaped not by knowledge but by our thought. Intellect discusses what intuition discovers.

13

The Voice of GOD

Paul, Samuel, Barnabas, Abraham, Mathias, Moses

Occasionally, GOD speaks in an audible voice, sometimes through a Prophet, or lot. There is no misunderstanding because you're clear on what to do.

Anoint Paul and Barnabas for the work I have done for them.

There're many people GOD called expressly to their Purpose, Samuel, Saul, Abraham, Moses, Paul, Peter, and many others.

Understand that, GOD has the prerogative to speak to you via any means HE deems appropriate. This approach is usually preferred especially when there're many equally qualified people but GOD in HIS wisdom elevating you before everyone and passing to you the mantle of the office.

Look at Joshua, without the open endorsement, many people like Aaron, Miriam, Gershom, Eleazer, Bezaleel and the likes are equally suitable choices.

Even for Elisha, Paul, Barnabas, Samuel, these people were not the next in line by the operation of the system set up by man, but they overtook others and no dissenting voice because it was GOD that made the choice.

This is a means of knowing the Will of GOD but it is by no means the only way.

When GOD speak whether through the audible voice or through the prophet, you can be rest assured that it is a possibility that still needs your cooperation to manifest into reality.

Don't be deceived into believing that because GOD said it; then it is automatic. Even after GOD called everything to being in Gen. 1, nothing was visible as it were, until Adam, the Man, worked it to life Gen. 2: 5.

Believing in what GOD said about you is by working it out not by confessing it. You can never think the Will of GOD to life, even GOD didn't do that.

Exercise:

GOD said something concerning you some years ago but up till now, the thing has not come to fruition, what can you do to expedite the fulfilment of prophecy?

When does doing something to aid the fulfilment of prophecy amounts to self-help?

Perfect Timing

Time and Chances happens to them all

Of what benefit is knowing what to do but not knowing when to do it?

The concept of Timing is so important that the very first thing GOD created in Genesis is Time. Timing ensures orderliness. You are a Soul that predates your earthly existence. You were born at the appropriate Time, when the Time was right for what you carry, you became.

Out of everything GOD created, the only thing HE didn't give Man authority over is Time.

When we choose to do things at our convenience, we may miss out on the cosmic time.

There is no individualism of time; we only have the individuality of personality. Everyone has approximately the same 24hrs a day, but not everyone is the same at each 24hrs. The only power you have over time is how you use it; you don't have power over when it comes.

How To Know the Perfect Timing

There're 3 ways to know the best time for the assignment GOD has mandated you with.

Number one: The time is perfect when GOD says so

Number two: the Time is right when your body says not

Number three: the Time is ripe when it follows the 3-5year rule.

Number one: WHEN GOD SAYS SO.

The art of perfect timing has everything to do with knowing the difference between Dedication and the actual Performance. You would always be on time when you are in time; when you are dedicated to a thing, the exact moment for performance will naturally reveal itself.

GOD doesn't just throw anyone out of the blue; a man of the moment probably spent many nights getting there *anonymous*. *Preparation* precedes *Presentation*, without your dedication, GOD won't dedicate you. You must go through the NIGHT time to your DAY, without studious dedication to something in silence; you become accidental discharge.

You don't wait for it; you don't walk into it; you work into it. Mt.25. If GOD showed you your Purpose, you must take the responsibility of dedicating yourself to that thing GOD had shown you while waiting for the day of your commissioning. You may not know the appropriate timing but when you commit yourself to that thing GOD shows you, and you are sensitive, you won't miss the 'when'.

The Bible says that the body wars against the Will of GOD meaning that whatever the body wants, the opposite of that thing is the Will of GOD for you.

When you think of doing something but your body wants you to do it now; just postpone it; if however, your body says later, just do it immediately.

Whatever your body wants you to do, just do the opposite and see how you're growing in the will of GOD for your life.

This has to do with how long you exercise patience or forebear with something that is not giving you the expected return so as not to waste your life on pursuing a dead lead and also you don't give up too early.

3 – 5 years rule has its foundation in the Bible. In Luke 13: 7, Jesus talked about a man that planted a fig tree in his garden; 3 years after the fig tree was expected to start fruiting, it hadn't. The keeper of the garden begged for one more year to be given to the tree before the decision to cut it down.

From the parable, the maximum a fig tree is expected to take without being cut down is 5 years.

Year 1	Establishing a good root system
Year 2 – 4	Fruiting and fruit ripening
Year 5	Grace period

Even if you don't know when to move on from waiting for something without wasting your time, the Bible has given you the hint. GOD would be worried if you are at the same level waiting for something for a year without a tangible fruit. If HE forgives you for not justifying the effort on you, the second year, HE expects you to start fruiting. The most HE would bear with you is 3 years and after that, you may be cut down.

For most people, Year 1 (the year of establishing a good rooting system) is usually age 30. At this age, you are expected to have found your Purpose in life and be committed to it.

This is in line with most people in the Bible. Jesus, John the Baptist, Joseph, Daniel, Saul, David, Ezekiel in Number 4, you cannot enter the office of priesthood until you are 30 years old.

The cheat code you can use is to make sure you commit yourself to that thing which you believe it is the 'Will of GOD' for you and to always ensure that you don't remain at a stage for at most 3 years and a level for at most 5 years.

Exercise:

What do you think is the limitation of 3 – 5year rule?
What is the difference between dedication and performance?
For how long should you forbear with something or someone to change before you move on in life?

"Until we can manage time, we can manage nothing else."

Peter F. Drucker

SECTION 3

162

The price for Wisdom is Humility; the price for knowledge is diligence; the understanding price is rumination.

Humility makes you see that you don't know it all and also grants you illumination to the secret things of life.

How To Know You're Walking in The Will of God

When you're working the Will of GOD, you will know. When you're doing what you are made for; your life begins to make meaning. You begin to crave for something beyond yourself; you begin to notice that your heart beats synchronously with your act. You now have joy and satisfaction that you've never experienced before.

Nobody that ever find Purpose wish for a better experience. It is the utmost and purest feeling anyone can have. It is the only feeling that you fear not about tomorrow nor death.

Your life has no meaning until it is lived for Purpose.

You will always find these characteristics in the life of those that are working out their Purpose. Those that have found one thing gives meaning to every other thing of the lives.

1. You're punching above your weight

If GOD send you or called you and you did not question your standing, your ability, your worth. If you do not ask sincerely, who am I to go before Pharaoh or to bring out the Israelis from Egypt, you have not found your purpose.

If we look at it; by all human calculations, Moses should be the last person, GOD should consider in setting the Israelites free. There're capable, strong, charismatic, knowledgeable and acceptable to the whole congregation in the camp, yet GOD left them and went as far as to diaspora to call someone who knows nothing about the custom and the tradition of the people. Moses didn't even know their GOD, yet he's the chosen one.

Gideon's family was inconsequential of the smallest tribe in Israel yet, it's he that delivered the whole nation. David wasn't thought good enough for anything good, even by his own father. Samuel was a son of Mr. nobody who rose to become the last theocratic head in Israel.

There're countless examples to cite of how people who were ordinary in their own eyes, achieve great feat.

GOD is in the habit of using 'ordinary people' for extra-ordinary things 1Cor. 1: 27 – 29.

Ordinary people have nothing to lose and everything to gain doing GOD's bidding.

I remembered my first job as a personal assistant to one notable man as a young graduate. I would receive calls on his behalf, make call, take minutes, manage his calendar and his correspondence et. cetera. I remembered receiving a call from someone from the Presidency to invite my boss for a meeting with the President, I remembered setting up meetings with eminent people and captains of industries. I remember when an eminent person who presided over board of notable organizations called me to request for a favour from me because he didn't want to call my boss.

I could enter anywhere when I carry his message, I could see kings without delay when I was on his errand.

I never knew the import of this privilege until the day I saw his banker in person. He was surprised so much that he queried if truly I was who I said I was (even though my boss just introduced me to him and left the two of us to finalize some arrangement). I affirmed and questioned why he seemed surprised. He answered that he thought I was somehow bigger than this.

Yes, I was. Not I, but the person behind me cast a shadow so big that makes me seem larger than life.

This is what happens when you decide to work out your purpose. Your purpose is not your work but GOD's assignment for you on this earth.

You will know you're in GOD's plan for your life when you're achieving what you never thought possible. You look at your impact, it far outweighs your size.

It doesn't matter what you are, it doesn't matter your status, your age, your qualification: it doesn't matter, you; if it is GOD assignment, then He is behind you casting a shadow; that is what people see, not you.

The only thing you can do is to surrender yourself more to be used by HIM after you've returned all the glory.

INSPIRATION

When you're working out your Purpose, even your Night time that's supposed to be a period of being alone, a moment of solitude, a period of being forgotten, isolated and rejected, becomes a period of fellowship with the comforter that teaches you what to do.

It's not only results that guarantee you're working out your Purpose; Ideas, Insights, Inspirations and Information you enjoy give a better judgement.

When you work on your Purpose, you attract the 'energy', the 'atmosphere' that creates and sustains everything you see on this earth and HE works with you Rom. 8: 28. That is HIS purpose and the GOD left HIS Spirit right here on earth, to fellowship and inspire anyone that has decided to go about the Father's Business Prov 7: 12, 15, 22-30.

You may not be achieving great results as expected for someone working with GOD, don't despair. As long as in that period of 'nothingness' when everything is dark, void and formless when you are forgotten and alone in the desert of life, tested and tempted, even if nobody thinks highly of you; if Ideas, Information, Insights and Inspiration keeps you up, then HIS Spirit is with you.

The presence of HIS Spirit is a pointer that you're walking in HIS Will; even if you're not making the desired progress, and you feel like you're living in the Night time of Life.

Night time is the period of little or no commensurate result to show for your efforts, it is by no means, a period of inactivity.

There can be no Day without Night because Night is:

N – New

I – Inspiration/Information/Insight/Idea

G – Given/Granted

H – Him/ Her

T – To

And Day is

D – Do

A – As

Y – Yearned

You cannot be what GOD had made you to be without HIS leading, without HIS Spirit speaking to you and giving you, Ideas, Insights, Inspiration and forming you from inside, to become what you have been made to be.

When you're operating in your divine mandate, you'd go through this moment, your wilderness years, months or weeks, but you're coming out with Inspiration, Insight, Idea, that the Spirit of GOD has implanted into you which you'd work out in the DAY.

That is why the Night time is made. GOD started HIS creative work from the NIGHT. JESUS could not have performed HIS purpose on earth without going through the wilderness. Moses, the fugitive, became bold as the result of what he saw in the wilderness.

When you are working out the seeds in your garden, the Spirit of GOD would be hovering over you, seeding Ideas, Inspirations, Insights in your heart.

This is what differentiate those working out their garden from those working out their lust. The dryness, the lack of result you're experiencing now is only meaningful when you have the Spirit of GOD seeding Inspiration into you. It is only that you know if you're going through a Trial or going into a Trap.

2. You're at REST

There's this inexplicable confidence and boldness in you when you're working out your garden that you can't die nor perish Is. 38, Phi 1: 23&24, Job 1: 12.

Tell me, which devil is stupid enough to stand against GOD's work or undermine HIM?

Except if purpose-driven individual deliberately court death or die a fool's death, death doesn't have any right over such a person.

The person working his garden is too busy to pay attention to frivolity as death because as long as he's working his garden, he's becoming indispensable to GOD here on earth.

Haunting Spirit, Fear of the unknown, Lack of courage, are all the afterwards of digressing from GOD's plan and Purpose. When you're doing what GOD has made you for, you carry not only HIS

Inspiration, but also have the confidence that HE is by your side.

3. People would come to you.

As the light of the world, when you live out your Purpose (shine), people and even kings would come to your light Matt. 5: 14. One way to know you are walking in the purpose of GOD, even though this is not definitive, is that people would come to you.

People came to David, People went to Jesus, immediately Elisha returned, the other sons of prophet came to him. If you are doing the work of GOD and people are not looking for you, then I doubt if what you carry is GOD's message or yours.

4. You are focus and consistent.

When you have found your Purpose, every other thing becomes uninteresting. You don't come face to face with your Purpose and be distracted by other things.

Trying to do many things at the same time, being drifted by what is in vogue, indefiniteness of Purpose, inconsistency, loss of desire, procrastination, are all signs that you have not found your Purpose yet. If you keep changing what you want to be every time, it means you have not found what you should be.

Purpose is a natural vim, drive and force that keeps you glue to an ever-refreshing desire. you never loss interest in it, not minding if you have to do it repetitively.

5. **You're motivated every time**

You don't need to be cajoled, to be prompted before you commit to your Purpose. In fact, you would always find a way to do it even if it takes denying yourself of certain life exigencies.

Time stops when you do what you're called to do and no opposition could stand in your way. You do it not for pecuniary reason, you do it because you are part of something bigger than you. You feel needed not needy.

6. **You Always know what to do**

Another very important sign post on your way to fulfilling destiny is clarity. You always know what to do. You're never stranded nor run out of idea.

You will notice that even if you are struggling with idea but when you take a break, when you allow the Spirit of GOD to speak to you, a new light, new idea would dawn on you, and idea would spring forth from nowhere.

It is like you have an invisible and unfathomable depth, inexhaustible wealth that you can recess to, to ferret out ideas.

Fulfilling destiny is not that hard. Nobody teaches a dog to bark, it just barks effortlessly. Every fiber of you is knitted to be that person you have been made to be. Fulfilling destiny is as easy as being yourself. Living out one's Purpose is the easiest and the most rewarding thing anybody can do.

It is far more difficult and unrewarding to be another person than to be your true self. When you decide to become you, everything just falls into place.

Your number one responsibility is to set yourself in line with these conditions set below. Feel free to read through them and you will be amazed how simple to achieve greatness.

You must kill impatience.

Patience is a mental and emotion strength to wait through a process or to allow a course to run its natural course. You have heard it said that Patience is a virtue, you bet it is.

One of the most difficult things to do is to sit by and do nothing. Patience is difficult when the ego is present. Patience is not irresponsibility, but it is about upholding the sanctity and the integrity of a process. Patience requires a great deal of self-control, emotional stability and faith.

Having Patience is not about being docile, it is not about being passive; it is about being calm and clear-headed during intense moments, it is about the ability to handle pressure, the fortitude to take a stand even when you've to stand alone, the equanimity not to be agitated, it is about the demonstration of faith not in oneself but in a higher power. Patience is a fruit of the Spirit that every would-be leader must have.

Patience is not against taking initiative. Patience seeks to satisfy these 3 basic conditions before acting and they are:

Is the power or right to act on behalf been delegated?

Is the result of delay too costly to be remedied by the person you're acting on behalf of?

Can you act on the person's behalf?

Patience is not a weakness; it is a virtue. That you can control yourself means you have gain mastery over self and it won't be long before you're giving mastery over others.

What you cannot wait for to have; you don't have the temperance to manage.

1Sam. 13: 13.

You must remain humble.

Maybe you have heard it being said that humility doesn't take anything from you but always add to you. JESUS in Matt. 5: 5 said that blessed are the meek, for they shall inherit the earth, meaning that what strength cannot get you, humility would drop it at your laps. The best things of this world are accessed by those that come down not the tallest. It is not by power; it is not by might; but by my Spirit says the Lord Zach 4: 6. As it had been pointed out in this book that you can only access to the Divine through humility.

Look at the representation of Man again represented overleaf:

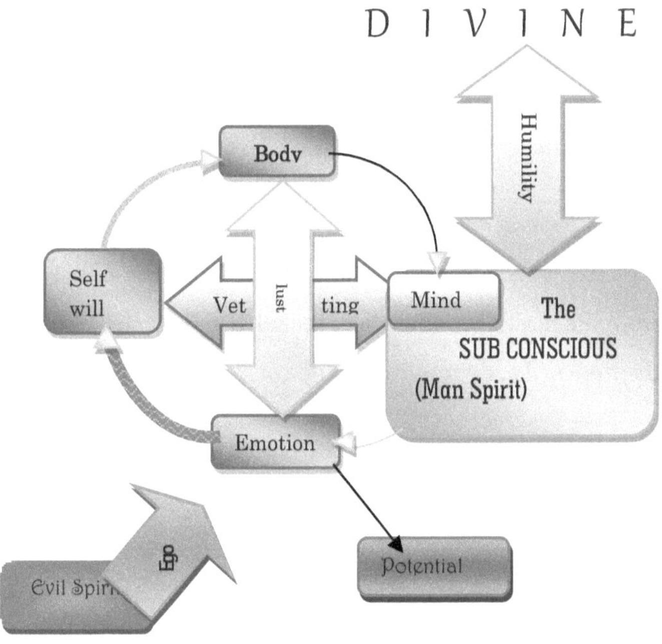

You can see that the only thing that keeps you from drifting toward evil spirits is the same thing that keeps you connected to GOD; it is humility.

You must be able to survive out of the limelight:

Can you stay outside of the limelight? Can you survive a moment in solitude? If you cannot, then you cannot fulfill destiny. This is because you would always elevate people's opinions over GOD's thoughts for your life.

Sometimes, being out of the limelight is GOD calling you to have a destiny-encountering discussion with HIM. GOD called Jacob to a solitary place, the same thing happened to Abraham, to Joseph, to Moses, to every who is who in the Bible.

Everyone must pass through the desert to their glorious city. Before the Day, there comes the Night.

Take a look at most living organisms, no matter how gregarious they are, when they are about to give birth, they usually withdraw from the group to somewhere secluded and somewhere away from their normal activity.

You need a nesting place when you are about to birth your destiny to reality.

JESUS would usually withdraw HIMSELF to a solitary place to know what is next on HIS assignment.

You need to go on a pilgrimage and withdrawal from people to reconnect back to your real self and your Purpose. You find yourself only in a place of silence.

Mind you, the solitary place is not just a physical place but it might be a place inside of you. As long as you can silence every worry, silence every voice to hear the still small voice in your heart.

You can do so on the altar of prayer while studying the Bible, when worshipping when fasting, or just sit still and open your heart to receive.

The most important thing is to free your mind from what the world is saying so that you can hear what GOD is saying.

Let go of fear

You cannot become what GOD has made you to be with fear as your guide. Fear shifts your focus from GOD to you and what HE is doing to what might never happen. Fear severe you from GOD and also from your Purpose Gen.3: 10.

Fear by default is a limiting factor. What you see and believe; that you may become. What Fear does is make you become something less than what you'd have become. It starts by making you doubt what you see with your unlimited spiritual eye and makes you believe what you can see with your limited physical eyes.

Fear is not the opposite of Faith. Both Fear and Faith act on what they believe: while one believes beyond what his physical limitation can do; the other believes in what only the physical limitation can do. In other word, Faith believes in what GOD says, fear believes in every other thing.

Let go of human idolatry

Human idolatry is accepting other people's opinions about something of interest without question. When you accept someone as the final authority over something of concern to you, that you surrender your reasoning and decision-making process to that person, you may never fulfil your destiny.

Fulfilling destiny is not for babes, it takes maturity (responsible person) to mount up the throne.

You might have heard it being said that the voice of the people is the voice of GOD. This is a lie from hell. The voice of the people is the voice of the people; the voice of GOD is the voice of GOD, don't confuse the two. Even if GOD speaks to you through anyone, you still have to discern.

You must also be able to let go of your family.

Some people love you so much that they don't want you to fulfill your purpose.

I don't know why but I've noticed that those who love you and take responsibility for your wellbeing are the ones who usually constitute the major impediments to your Purpose Mk. 8: 33, Lk. 2: 49.

Adam lost the garden because he could not say no to Eve. Until you are ready to draw a line for your GOD and your destiny which no family member can cross, you are not going far in destiny Matt. 19: 29, Matt 10: 34-39.

Love your wife, take care of your family, honour your parent but they must not stop you from fulfilling your purpose.

It is normal if they don't believe what you see about yourself, you won't be the first person and neither would you be the last. Joseph's brethren didn't believe him despite his good effort to make them see. David didn't waste his time trying to prove to his biological father that he too could be king. He lost his cool when his brother wanted to shut him off his calling and his purpose.

Despite being told that her child would be Messiah, Mary still wanted to be controlling of the child's life. Peter married but left his wife and everyone to go after destiny.

Anyone who wants to dictate how you go about your Purpose would rob you of your destiny.

Destiny is a personal commitment; don't make it a community one.

The paraphernalia of the office must not appeal to you more than the impact.

One of the factors that distinguish Purpose from Dream is the 'why' behind the decision. When you want to be something or someone because of the privilege that it offers, because of self-aggrandizement and ego, that is not Purpose but a self-contrived dream.

You cannot expect GOD to commit to what HE's not the author. GOD resists the proud but gives grace to the humble. When you want to be anything to consume it on your selfish nature, you're proud.

When you compare Gehazi and Joshua together, you will see that while Joshua had the Spirit (desire for service) Gehazi had the lust (the privilege of the office).

The thing that set Elisha apart from other sons of Prophets even though he was the least among them was that he wasn't after the title, not after the power nor influence but was about GOD and the people.

That thing you call your Purpose, what motivates you? What do you want to see achieved? Is your heart pure? Do you see the scepter as a symbol of power, a symbol of affluence and control? A means to find your voice, and prove a point to your haters and doubters? Do you see your new office to promote your welfare, that of your family, close associates, or your parochial interest?

Despite what the rod could do, Moses never used it to take vengeance or as a show off before Pharaoh. The only time Moses used the rod to satisfy anything else aside from GOD's glory, he lost his destiny Num. 20:12.

GOD is not against you using the gift HE has given you to protect yourself when the need arises but you must never use it to promote yourself but GOD. When you use your gift to promote GOD, GOD would in return promote you.

Have you thought how easy it is for David to have lost his Destiny and become the villain?

What do you think would have become of him, had he killed Saul the moment he had the opportunity?

David would not only have lost the throne to Jonathan, but he'd have become the number one enemy of the state.

Had JESUS turned stone into bread to satisfy his hunger, we wouldn't have saviour today.

Samson could not live long enough to fulfill his destiny because he was busy using the gift to fight his battle.

When GOD gives you any gift or Talent, GOD doesn't expect you to use it to prove a point nor advance yourself over others but to bring about the establishment of HIS purpose(glory) on earth.

When you're motivated by the power, the affluence, the glory that your gift carries, you tend to misuse it and would eventually lose it before you can fulfil the purpose for it.

You must be ready to let go of any success for your Call.

When you're down, it's easier to surrender yourself to your Destiny; after all, you have nothing to lose. But it is very difficult to yield to any call when everything seems to be going well. Imagine being promoted to a position you have hoped for, for many years, only for the Spirit of GOD to tell you to resign that position and move to a place you know anything about.

I was in that situation, believe me, it wasn't easy. You'd want to rebuke that voice; you'd pretend you don't know how GOD speaks again; you may even rebuke the voice as satanic.

When you study the life of great men in the Bible, you'd find instances that suggest GOD called them when they were well and doing.

Abraham was at the stage when he thought life couldn't be better when GOD called him to leave his people to a place, he knew nothing about. If you're Abraham's friend and he came to tell you that he was leaving a striving business to a place he knows nothing about, what are you going to think? Abraham, my friend is crazy?

It also happened later that Abraham went down to Egypt against GOD's plan but he was successful and he became rich, how do you convince someone like that, that Egypt wasn't the right place for him and for the person to go back to Canaan where hunger almost killed him?

Elisha was a big-time farmer. Imagine having 24 cows to spare at the time when the whole continent was just coming out from 42 months of famine. This is by no means a mean achievement. What he had, Ahab, the king did not have. Elisha was up there.

JESUS did not come to Peter to call him to his destiny when things were tough for him, when he was struggling to make ends meet. But immediately after Peter got the much-eluded breakthrough, Destiny came calling Lk. 5: 10.

This GOD is wonderful, isn't HE? Only HIM understands why HE does the things HE does sometimes; all we can do is trust and obey

HIM.

You have to be ready to let go of any apparent success when Destiny comes calling.

Work on yourself

I find it hard to understand the arguments of some people. They say GOD saw them the way they are when HE called them so they're not willing to change. They hold on to unhealthy behavior and bad family tradition.

Abraham was the son of a terrible father. Terah was an idol worshipper. Gideon's father was the chief priest of Baal, and Moses was a proud person who had anger issues. Peter was fearful, Nathaniel was obstinate; all of them once had one issue or the other they were struggling with before GOD called them to their purpose. They didn't say that GOD saw them that way and so they'd remain that way.

The only people that didn't work on themselves while on their Purpose eventually were disgraced out of their Destiny.

Take, for example, Saul. Saul had always been someone who courted people's attention, so he was an attention freak and would do anything to be in the good book of the people. This is what later becomes his albatross that made him to lose his throne. Because of wanting to satisfy the people, he offered a sacrifice he shouldn't have.

Another example is Judas Iscariot. The guy loves money so much that he stole from JESUS. Instead of him to repent when he was caught stealing from the purse, he did not. He consoled himself that JESUS knew him before HE called him. JESUS knew that he could not do without money. At the end of the day, it was the same money that made him sell his master for 30 pieces of silver and the same money was used to bury him.

Is there any habit, any custom, any weakness you're currently grappling with right now? That GOD calls you into your Destiny doesn't give you the liberty to continue in that. You cannot be in grace and say sin should abound(paraphrased).

Your Purpose is the reason you were made is not an approval of sort. Don't confuse it together. You can live all your life in your Purpose and still end up in hellfire if you don't settle that presumptuous sin in you.

David nearly lost the kingdom because of Absolom the child of Abigail the wife of Naban, who died mysteriously after David and Abigail exchanged secret meetings. David even killed to marry Bathsheba. In all of these, David didn't stop working on himself and never justified his weakness.

The moral is that, that GOD is using you doesn't exempt you from being perfect.

Your knowhow

Trust in the Lord with all thine heart, and lean not on your understanding.

There's this story of a king's officer who overheard Elisha telling the king that the nation would witness a total turnaround from hunger to affluence in 24 hours. He, trying to impress the king that he knows his onion cast aspersion on Elisha's word, 2king 7.

Lot, when he was about to leave Abraham, he chose the best place around for himself not knowing that there was already a death sentence in that place, Gen. 13: 10.

Lot lost everything he had laboured for in 50 years in a single day. All because he didn't reckon with GOD's factor in his life. Lot, was a good man, but died as an animal.

Yes, GOD doesn't usually interfere in our system and protocol but whenever HE does, our system has no choice but to fall in line.

When GOD tells you to do something, don't try to rationalize it. As long as you're sure it is GOD that is speaking, just go ahead and do it. Put in your utmost best.

At 100 years, when the angel of GOD told Abraham that Sarah his wife would give birth to his son according to time of life. Immediately, Abraham, who has stopped being with her as man with woman, knew her and that was what became Isaac.

Assuming now that Abraham did not do the needful, it doesn't matter what the angel said, Sarah would not conceive. It was not GOD's intention to have an immaculate conception but a child from the copulation of both Abraham and Sarah.

You cannot become what GOD has made you to be depending on your strength, wisdom, training, and know-how, neither can GOD perform what HE wants to do without your input.

You need God and GOD needs you. You and GOD are mutually dependent on one another.

28 Reasons People Fail in Fulfilling Their Calling

Have you heard that destiny is a mirage? You cannot fulfill destiny if any of these are present in your life: as small and innocent they may look, they have recked the destiny of many powerful people and reduced mighty men to mere crumbs.

Procrastination – Lk. 9: 59 – 62, Jm. 4: 17 Prov. 24: 30 -34

Impatience –Prov. 21: 5, Gal. 5: 22 – 23, Ps. 37: 7 – 8.

Seeking people's approval — Eph 6: 6, Gal.1:10

Lack of Discipline – Heb. 12: 11, 1 Cor. 9: 27, Prov. 5: 23

Lack of self-belief –Hab. 2:4, Matt. 17: 20

Too money-conscious –Mt. 6: 24, 1Tim. 6: 6 –10, Lk. 12:15.

Vengefulness –Deut. 32: 35, Ps. 94: 1, Is. 35: 4, Rm. 12: 19.

Immorality or sexual indiscipline – 1Cor. 6: 18, Lev. 18: 22, Rev. 21: 8, Matt. 19: 9, Matt. 5: 27 – 28.

Feeling of arrival/egoistic –Jm. 4:6, Pro.16:18, Mt. 5: 5.

Lack of commitment/lack of diligence – Prov 22: 29, 2 Pet. 1: 10, Col. 3: 23.

Selfishness or self-centeredness – Prov. 11: 25, Lk. 22: 27

Lack of integrity – Prov. 11: 3, Prov. 28: 6, Deut. 25: 15, Pro 14:34

Lack of discernment – Luk. 12: 54 – 56, Ps. 82: 5.

Lack of Joy/ murmuring – 1Cor. 10: 10

Wrong association – Ps. 1, Prov. 27: 17, 1Cor. 15: 33

Lack of respect for Parent & Husband – Ex. 20: 12, Eph. 5: 33.

Not showing love to wife – Eph. 5: 25

Disobedience – Deut. 28: 1 – 68.

Not taking care of your body/mind – 1Cor. 3: 16, Rm. 12: 1.

Besetting sin – Heb. 12:1, Ps. 19: 13.

Covetousness – Ex. 20: 17, Lk. 12: 15, Eph. 5: 5, Jm. 4: 3.

Complacency – Rev. 3: 15 – 16, Amos 6: 1, Is. 32: 9, 1 Cor. 9: 24.

Taking offence in GOD

Grieve the HolySpirit – Pandering towards fear as

against Faith.

Lack of Entrepreneurship (know the road to the market)

Lack of Management (don't just do your part, make others do their part also)

Final thought

It is never too late to be who GOD had made you to be. Don't think you have outgrown your purpose on earth, no. That you are still alive is a testament that your purpose is still alive. Don't allow pride, guilt, lack of self-belief, low self-esteem, or physical, social, and economic situations to rob your life of meaning. GOD still wants you to bear fruit, that is why HE had not hewed you down. Jacob's life had no meaning at 80 years and he was not worried about it. But in 20 years, Jacob's life took a dramatic turn. Someone that had no change of cloth, no money, no means of transportation but 20years on, had gotten 4 wives, 11 children, cattle and wealth in abundance that he had to divide them into camps. Jacob, a nonentity, had become so rich that he could afford to give out 220 goats, 220 sheep, around 50 camels, 50 cows, and 30 donkeys. Jacob had become a multi-millionaire by the world standard of today. A person that had nothing to his name except wives and children 6years earlier had this massive turnaround.

Life of a Professional Boxer

You can learn some life lessons from professional boxing bout. It doesn't matter if a boxer is being beaten blue and black, his corner will always root for him. You will see that at the end of each round, when the boxer returns to the corner, he's being treated as a king. One person would bring a stool for him to sit, another gives him water or electrolyte to restore his sapped energy, another person examining his face, rubbing something on it, another would be massaging his neck and shoulder, another dishing out tactical advice. All of these happen in between the rounds.

As long as the boxer keep returning to his corner during the break, he can still win the fight.

Ask yourself, do you return to your corner as often as at when needed? Do you take instruction from your corner? Do you see any need for it at all?

Yes. You have been with your corner for quite some time now, preparing and perfecting strategy for the fight; do you know that your corner can never give you every detail to win the fight during the preparation for the fight?

Some tactics would become needed as the fight progresses. That is the benefit of always returning to your source.

Your corner is the Master tactician himself, JESUS. HE with the HolySpirit are sure bet that you'd win the belt. The greatest undoing of many is that they don't return to their corner and even when they do, they don't carry out the instruction given by their corner.

ABOUT THE AUTHOR

Ade Omooba is the President of Kingdemmie International, a non-governmental organization with a mandate to help people struggling to find purpose and identity in life, those who had almost given up on life; find their feet in life including those who are going through midlife crisis.

He is also an inspirational writer/speaker and more importantly, a yielded vessel drawing people to GOD's original plan.

I would love to hear from you, please send an e-mail to

adewumiomooba@gmail.com